Below the Belt

For Jill
with my love
and belated thanks for the washing up

Below the Belt

Clement Freud

Robson Books

The author would like to thank the editors and proprietors of *Punch* magazine and of *High Life* for permission to include material previously published by them.

FIRST PUBLISHED IN GREAT BRITAIN IN 1982 BY ROBSON BOOKS LTD., BOLSOVER HOUSE, 5–6 CLIPSTONE STREET, LONDON W1P 7EB. COPY-RIGHT © 1982 CLEMENT FREUD

British Library Cataloguing in Publication Data

Freud, Clement
  Below the belt.
  1. Food
  I. Title
  641.3   TX353
  ISBN 0–86051–199–5

Printed in Great Britain by Biddles Ltd., Guildford

Contents

BILL OF FARE   vii

LOOKING BACK A BIT   1

VERY WELL, BREAD   16

COMMONERS AND KINGS   32

IDEAL WORLD   58

MONOMANIAS   74

PROFESSIONALS' TOUCHES   92

ROUND THE CLOCK   112

ROUND THE WORLD   128

ALL THE YEAR ROUND   146

INDEX   169

Bill of Fare

A generous selection of the delicious ideas to be found in *Below the Belt*. The instructions and information necessary to prepare these dishes and drinks will be found on the pages indicated.

Breakfast dishes

Eggs Benedictine   62
Kippers   114
Champagne sausages   103–4
Freud's Improved Sausage   148

Starters

Avocado with lemon juice and sugar   76
Poor Man's Caviare   132
Smoked mackerel mousse   53–4
Pasta with cream and ham sauce   98

Soups

Borsch	132–3
Broth	51–2
Celery soup	88
Cockie leekie	129
Tourin aux tomates	47
Vichyssoise	97, 147

Fish

Poached Canadian salmon	101
Kulibiaki (fish in pastry)	133
Russian baked fish	133

Main course dishes

Fondu Bourguignon	49
Calf's liver hotpot	88
Chicken à la Freud	61
Chicken in cider	79
Lemon chicken	75
Tarragon chicken	80
Szechwan duck	136
Haggis	129
Hamburgers	140–3
Meat loaf	133
Paella	154
Piroshki ('Little pie')	133
Pork cheese	126
Roast grouse	62–3
Roast turkey with stuffing etc.	163–4

Sauces

Bread sauce	164
Hollandaise sauce	14
Mayonnaise	87
Tapps sauce (pungent Eastern chutney)	167

Vegetables

Brussels sprouts	165
Potatoes: new	101–2, 126
baked	121–2
Ratatouille	64, 70

Salads

Lettuce and walnut	143
Ham and potato	104
Rice	157
Watercress and corn	63

Savouries

Chanterelles on toast	64
Cheese fondu	49
Egg and anchovy toast	126
Kidneys on toast	149
Welsh rarebit	27

Puddings

Fruit salad	26
Lemon ice-cream	76
Vanilla ice-cream with chocolate sauce	98
Peach Melba	60
Summer pudding	148

Drinks and Beverages

Citron pressé	75
Banana milk shake	68
Grown-up's banana milk shake	149
Kir	63
Potable peach	62
Miss Wrackham's ruin	7
Mulled wine	12

Cocktails

Bloody Maria   145
Bullshot   51
Godfather   153
Lolita   145
Margarita   145
Tequila sunrise   145
Tequila sunset   145

Sundries

Home-made bread   17
Fried bread   116
Melba toast   60
Scones, plain and fruit   123–4, 131
Salted almonds   44

CHAPTER ONE

Looking back a bit

MILK TEETH

First recollections of gastronomy
Were when I squinted down the tablecloth
And saw the junket move in empathy
With custards, jellies, brawn—all porringered
In Georgian silver, burnished by the maid.
(That maid had buttocks like a granary,
And habits that were looked on with askance
In those commencement du siècle *days.)*
And we drank wine from Irish crystal glass;
The claret sold at twelve-and-six a case,
We ended meals with vintage Sercial—
Began them with a glass of Burgundy,
White—as the inside of young Basil's thigh
(Though not, one hardly needs to state, as warm).
Basil did knives, which left him much free time.

On Sundays when the Robinsons came by
Just after matins, for a stirrup cup,

Delilah Watts made gorgonzola straws,
With flaky pastry spiked with paprika.
And that old drone, despite advancing years,
Had a relationship with Seth the Boots.
Of which old Sergeant Watts, ex-railway guard
(Now dead and buried by the copper beech
In the north corner of the cemetery—
The grave with marble-stone; tooled with gold,
The legend, telling all who chance to read
That William Watts is herein laid to rest
By his adoring wife) was not aware.
Nanny served tea in the night nursery,
The best Darjeeling in blue Wedgwood cups,
And Garibaldi biscuits, lemon cake,
Thin buttered Hovis with a plum preserve
That came from Bath by Carter Paterson.
Now, what the van-man did in nanny's room
We'll never know, though father one June night
Mistook the chamber where the nursemaid slept
For his own dressing-room and found them there.

So nanny had to leave; and father left
Soon afterwards, to live in Islington,
From where he sent us postcards of a shop
With bow-front window and embellished beams,
And shelves of liquorice and caramel,
Everton toffee, fudge and acid drops,
Turkish delight, nut cracknel, isinglass,
And, in a corner of the teak front door,
A notice asking Carter Paterson
To stay away or risk the consequence.

A Cornish woman came and took the place
Of nanny in the third floor nursery:
Young, widowed, comely, with an upper lip
On which, I swear, there grew more golden hair
Than graced the skin of Giles, my guinea-pig.

When I was eight, we moved to Harrogate;
Mother took rooms above a butcher's shop. . . .

There was a time when cooking was a profession; an honoured and respected calling and the cook who cooked for a King or a nobleman had a cook's cook—who cooked for the cook.

Nowadays, the cost of labour allows few households to employ a designated cook or indeed anyone at all, and as the quality of our basic food becomes ever more boringly standardised, so is it becoming increasingly important to teach the art of cookery to the ever-growing army of practitioners.

A plump chicken that strolled aggressively among the worms and cereals of a farmyard, pecking at a berry here, a batch of wild garlic there, was once a walking, clucking, self-contained delicacy. It needed no more than a quick twist of the neck at the age of 9 months, an expert pluck and dress, some tarragon leaves stuffed into its cavity, seasoned butter smeared on its outside and, irrespective of the oven temperature or the length of sojourn therein, the end product was memorable . . . especially so if it was basted at regular intervals. No more.

You just try that with its distant relative the muted, gelded, bemused, immobile battery chicken! An hour in the oven will give you no more than a muted, gelded, bemused, immobile roast battery chicken, instantly distinguishable from blotting paper by its shape and colour . . . and yet it is wrong to write off chicken simply because its unembellished taste is caused by its staggeringly unembellished life. Today's chicken is a challenge and rising to that challenge is the growing number of cookery schools designed to teach you to create Timbale des Oreilles de Cochon, Sauce Ravigotte from sows' ears.

The teaching of pure cookery—as opposed to tinkering in the kitchen with copper pans, silver-plated whisks and inlaid mahogany and teak chopping boards on the way to discovering some stunning napkin-folding technique—is a new growth industry.

3

There was a time when ladies learnt to cook on the way to being 'finished'. There is still a bit of that . . . but for every one paying £100 a week at social academies for the nicely-reared, there are a dozen who learn the trade at local authority evening classes.

What used to be 'domestic science' became 'home economics' and is now plain 'cooking', though home economics is an excellent support subject.

It used to be said that the French Minister of Education could look at his watch and know exactly what was being taught in every school in France. The great strength of cookery lessons at evening classes, and interest groups from young wives to lonely grannies, is the refreshing variety of the teaching and there is no cookery teacher who does not have something useful to impart.

Heaven knows, the Coq au Vin demonstration may not result in the classical confection they sell you at Maxims, but if you learn that, in cooking, wine must be boiled, spirits set alight and reinforced wine like sherry and port added at the last moment before serving, the lesson will not have been in vain.

And if a cookery lesson makes you think and experiment and, above all, read cookery books with discrimination and understanding, you are well on the way to expertise.

The important thing to remember is that with the exception of making sweets and biscuits, there is no absolute in cookery. Certainly, the classic way to make a Hollandaise sauce is with egg yolks, butter and a squeeze of lemon . . . but the great Escoffier decreed that you should add a few drops of Maggi meat extract (and suffered the contempt of his colleagues and the riches of Nestlés). I have seen it based on white sauce, made bland with thick cream (which is technically a sauce mousseline) and faked by boiling up the butter in a little water and whisking the mixture in a cold pudding basin; that is a good morning's work for any student and if, in the course of this, he learns how to use egg yolks to thicken oils and liquids, classic dishes from custard to mayonnaise are at his fingertips.

Perhaps the most useful part of the cookery school is not the interpretation of recipes but the general approach to the kitchen. In my youth I did an apprenticeship in the kitchen of a first-class hotel (all right, the Dorchester) and when I came home on my day off my friends, salivating, would say, 'Cook us something you've learnt.'

I hadn't learnt to cook anything. I had learnt to have an inbuilt feeling about when the baked potatoes would be ready to come out of the oven; I could 'pull' a soup as well as the next man ('pulling soup' means stirring the bottom of the pan as it thickens) though it took years to find out what actually went into the soup.

I found out . . . and have since taught others . . . that the best way to peel an onion is to cut it in half, lengthwise, and then remove the outside skin.

I discovered . . . and my friends took due note . . . that you peel hard-boiled eggs by cracking the shell all the way round the middle and when you have a belt of cracked shell, peel off a little of that belt and the two halves come away effortlessly.

And I was taught to chop and slice using the weight of the knife—therefore the part of the blade closest to the handle—rather than being fooled into the popular fallacy that a sawing motion with the sharp end is the way to do it.

I started work in a hotel kitchen at the age of 16 and with a few significant interludes I have been cooking odd meals ever since. I have never stopped learning and I doubt whether there is anyone who has ever produced a decent dish who could not teach me something.

If you see an advertisement for a cookery school or a cookery class, go and enroll . . . and if, in the fullness of time (after the first couple of hours), you feel that the teacher cannot teach you anything, think about opening up your own cookery school.

Now is the time for all good cooks to come to the aid of providing better parties.

*

I used to pity my school friends who went into the Army or the City for their inability to combine work with love. I was a romantic . . . and became an apprentice cook.

My friends would find girls, take them out and bore them to

distraction holding forth on subjects as compelling as .303 rifles, 'with profits' policies, or deposit accounts. They would then complain about the girl's early departure home.

I found no girls, mainly because I worked what would now be called 'unsociable hours', but I was pretty certain that when I did, my growing experience with pots and pipkins would achieve very much more than did their mundane small talk.

Admittedly, having intended to learn to do irresistible things with white truffles, partridge breasts, plovers' eggs and grape brandy, the wartime economy confined my culinary forays to sago, coley—which is an off-white fish—and margarine—about the only things that were not in short supply. But we of check trousers and proudly starched hats did with sago, coley and margarine things that had never before been attempted with those journeyman products; what is more, we did these things using the most eclectic utensils, from copper pans to French vegetable knives, not to mention sauteuses, mandolines, tammy cloths and pallets.

My first encounter with a real girl (a description which excluded sisters of school friends) was at a Christmas staff party. I forget her name, but remember that she worked in the linen room, was tall, thin and lived a very long way from a Tube station. I walked her home from the staff party and when we got to her house, she leaned down and I tried to kiss her mouth; I got her chin.

It seemed a disaster at the time, but on reflection it was not too bad for a first attempt. Certainly the girl was quite impressed, mentioning that she had never had anyone kiss her chin. The walk back seemed shorter.

I spent a lot of time and energy on that girl over the next few weeks, and realising that compulsive food was unavailable, other food unappetising, decided that drink would be my best chance of transforming her into something other than a tall, thin, distant and mildly bored recipient of a chin-peck. I read books in the library, but was steadily frustrated by maddening phrases such as 'also a suspicion of oriental roots' or 'then a few hours maceration in Mediterranean spices'.

One night I tried it with gin. I showed her that there was

6

nothing remotely suspicious about a young man of good family and dishonourable intentions giving a girl gin by drinking a glass or two myself . . . and passed out.

I never saw the linen room girl again . . . but the idea of a love potion to aid my romantic desires became increasingly attractive. Some inexpensive, easily obtainable concoction that would transform a cool collected female into a hot, frenzied, passionate octopus (I was looking only at the short term). In that seventeenth year of my life, I spent the days cooking war-time food, messing around with coley and sago and seeing what the odd bottle-ends of Moselle that came down from the restaurant would do for me.

In my state it was hard to tell. My thoughts were so deeply wrapped up in the expectation of love that any food or drink, or lack thereof, made me feel as I would have had my victim feel.

About a month after the gin episode, I heard on the grape-vine that a liftboy called Wrackham had a sister—and knowing what sort of a chap Wrackham was, there seemed every likeli-hood that Miss Wrackham might be the very person I was looking for. By that time I had a room in South Terrace with a gas ring. I took Miss Wrackham to a film and brought her home for 'supper'.

All was carefully and lovingly arranged; 'all' included a concoction described in a book by Norman Douglas which had lured a page-boy in a Berlin hotel into the most enjoyable *halbe stunde*. Hock and seltzer with a slug of apricot brandy served in a tall frosted glass, the rim rubbed with lemon peel and dried with caster sugar.

I offered to hang up Miss Wrackham's coat but she said it was all right and sat on the bed.

I cooked two fillets of coley on a bed of sago and she asked whether there were no chips; there were no chips. The conversa-tion lapsed and I looked deep into her eyes and said, 'I think I have something that will please you very much,' went out and brought in the frosted glasses of prepared hock and apricot brandy freshly topped with seltzer.

No book ever gives you the timing of a love potion. Should it

7

take effect as the liquor touches the lining of the stomach, or does it, like aspirins, take 20 minutes? I drank my glass and sat watching her for signs as she sipped bird-like from hers. It took less time than aspirins; to the best of my memory, about eight minutes, and if it was not all passion and tentacles, it was a very fair manifestation of acquiescence.

Later that evening, I offered her another glass and she said no, thanks, she must be going. I saw her to South Ken tube station, feeling like a satiated roué.

It was not until several weeks later, when I had irrevocably unbalanced my budget with wild purchases of apricot brandy, that I learnt from diverse colleagues that Miss Wrackham also performed on half pints of mild ale.

In fact, my former schoolfriends would probably have bowled her over with accounts of cleaning cap badges.

To Box 3072 Forum Magazine
Dear highly intelligent, excitingly different, exclusive, attractive, unkinky, shapely Taurean of 5ft 6in in her mid-thirties (looks younger).

I realise that the job specifications of the man for whom you are searching—and to whom you offer the full panacea of loyalty, fidelity, compassion and warmth—are going to be hard to fill, but I wonder whether I might not just qualify?

You seek someone who is 'honest, uncommitted, over 5ft 10in tall, educated, well-spoken, sensitive, fit, reasonably stable, beardless, non-smoking, animally chunky-but-slim, nature-loving, assertive, masculine, un-broke, un-circumcised, strictly hetero, possibly difficult, but not a sadistic or psychotic fella, 38–45 years, who knows what he wants'.

Let us start with the unarguable points in my favour:

I am possibly difficult. In fact I am more than possibly difficult and can produce many references to that effect. I am utterly uncircumcised and do not smoke; not ever. I am 5 ft 10 in, but would be considerably taller than that if I wore a hat or built-up shoes. (I don't . . . but if you are really excitingly different, I could give it a whirl. Also, I have a rather neat beard ... but if you really look less than mid-thirty and insisted on it, that could come off; it only went on to make me look over mid-thirty some years ago. I am educated ... who is not? and well-spoken; quite particularly well-spoken, actually.

About being animally chunky-but-slim; I am more chunky than slim and if I knew what you meant by being animally, I could work on that. I fail a bit on 'nature-loving' if that means I should prefer to listen to the first cuckoo in March than sip a glass of 1969 Louis Roederer Crystal Champagne.

I am un-broke ... note the first-class stamp on the envelope ... totally hetero (but for a rather ugly incident with a hotel pageboy when I was very young) and neither sadistic nor psychotic.

Regrettably, I just fail in the age range, being within muted shouting distance of your upper limit, but—like you—I look younger.

The problem about arranging a meeting between such excitingly different people as us is that clearly neither wants to disclose his/her identity before having had a chance to examine the other. I mean, if you were to send me a photograph and I recognised you as the lady in the flat downstairs who looks fifty if she looks a day and who is excitingly different only if one were expecting Raquel Welch, it would be a pretty ghastly waste of time.

On the other hand, if I sent you a photograph of myself, how would you know it had been taken since the war?

Here's what we will do.

If you feel that I might just qualify (remember: 5ft 10in, no taller, a beard, *over* 45 but otherwise ... according to specifications) let me give you a telephone number at which I will be each morning next week between 9.30 and 10.30 a.m. You will know me from my well-spoken, hetero, assertive voice and my possibly difficult, though not sadistic or psychotic, enunciation.

I usually call myself 'Jock' until I have got to know someone better, but as you make such a point of exclusivity, I shall answer to any élitist name ... shall we say Peverel, Gervaise —possibly Peregrine?

I look forward very much to hearing from you.

P.S. If someone else answers the telephone, it is likely to be my wife and I should appreciate it if you could ring off and try again later. (Naturally, if you recognise the telephone number and *are* my wife, I am sorry about this letter and about skipping the subject of 'commited'; but damn it, you aren't 5ft 6in—not unless you wear a hat, or built-up shoes.)

When my wife and I got married all those years ago, one of the pleasures of our life was to go out and buy things for the home: half a dozen plates from an antique shop in Frome; a dozen Finnish glasses from Heal's; eight teaspoons that looked as if they were gold from a stall in Portobello Road market . . . that sort of life-style seems to be a thing of the past.

Looking through the *Sunday Times* Colour Magazine, it was hard to miss an advertisement that promises to deny you all the fun of gently filling your derelict kitchen. For £29.95 they will send you 48 beautiful items of tableware, 12 attractive glasses and 44 pieces of stainless steel cutlery and if you rush off your cheque by Tuesday I expect they will chip in a horse-hair mattress and send André Previn to come and tune your television set.

On the illustration there is also an egg and a plateful of fruit salad which will not benefit from the 'allow 21/28 days for delivery' but I will let that pass.

What worries me is *who* is going to need all those things? I mean what on earth did they do at meal-times before the '104 useful items a home needs' arrived? I have met people who decided that their ash-trays were getting worn out and needed to be replaced but surely not the silver, the glasses *and* the crockery, all at the same time? I suppose it could be a package for the departing partner in a marriage break-up, especially if he is going to open a small hotel; he could make use of the '14 day trial please'. I wonder whether you have to wash it all up before you send it back?

Actually I was not going to write about that advertisement; it was another, a few pages on in the magazine, that caught my eye.

'Cook a total meal in one pan with no pressure,' said the heavy print and there was a picture of an outer saucepan in which there were three tiers of aluminium compartments holding respectively a chicken, potatoes and three vegetables, one above the other. Let me make it clear that if you want steamed chicken, steamed potatoes, steamed peas, steamed carrots and steamed courgettes, the Combined English Stores Direct Sales Heatmiser at £15.95 post-free has got to be better than using five pudding basins and a lot of foil. Let me also state that the saucepan itself, without the interior clutter, looks like a very sound piece of equipment—though I wish the advertisement would give the measurements; their only clue is that the three baskets 'rest on a ½-inch trivet'.

Frankly, the offer surprised me, because if there is one thing that we know about current eating habits, it is that the meat and potato and three veg meal, especially when all items are cooked in the same manner, is out.

Chinese takeaway is in. *Nouvelle cuisine*, which is about under-cooking, glazing with pastry brushes and cunning arrangement on plates, is in. English chefs with beards who have never been to France are in as are ladies who do interesting things with quails' eggs. Butter is in again and cream has reached a new high in acceptability, but a three-tier steamer, even one available in burnt orange at no extra cost, is a break-through; I say that because the company will have done its market research with care and the pot will sell like an insulated boot in a snowstorm.

I wonder what will happen to the device in the years to come because if there is another thing about which I know, it is that gadgets bought from Sunday supplement advertisements have a life-span of not very long.

On the first day you cook the very meal that is illustrated: steamed chicken in the bottom compartment, potatoes in the next, veg in the top. I expect they will tell you in the instructions that unless the chicken is very small and the potatoes enormous you will have to put them in at different times unless you like your chicken *aldente* or your potatoes steamed into submission.

Possibly—the picture did not show this very clearly—the

chicken was a midget or perhaps you cook chicken joints; what will be delicious is the sauce—the water which has been producing steam and is flavoured with the five tastes. Reduce this by boiling, add cream and *beurre manie* (which is butter into which you have massaged its own weight in flour) and you will have a great chicken and potato and carrot and courgette and pea soup, especially if you add salt and pepper. Boil it down and you get an impeccable white sauce.

After that I expect the aluminium trays will end up in the cupboard with the rotisserie grill and the angel cake tin and the wire biscuit stand—near the Tupperware jars, to the left of the sugar thermometer, by the icing nozzles. As for the saucepan, if it is as big as it looked in the picture it is going to come in very useful when the marmalade season starts or possibly—now that Spain is joining us in the EEC—every month. I never did quite understand why Seville oranges have so short a season but I am ready to believe, because of all that I hear at Westminster, that it has something to do with market forces.

If you do not go for your own marmalade—and I now buy mine at W.I. stalls so that we get a different taste every now and then—a huge saucepan is marvellously useful for any number of things: cassoulet, which is made with beans and sausage and pork and bits of goose in France. It is very good without goose, also.

You can use the pan for heating water when the boiler breaks down or make mulled wine for Christmas guests. Equal parts of wine and water still give the mull a slight kick but remember that you must boil the water with the sugar and the cinnamon, clove and nutmeg and put in the wine at the last moment, serve when the mixture is very hot and top up glasses of favoured adults with cheap spirits. Kids can drink the stuff as it is, though you can top up very young children's mull with extra water and sugar.

Someone, somewhere has got our Census form and I just hope that they are pleased with the answers. We certainly took a lot of trouble filling it in, trying to remember the date of the

Diploma in Dramatic Art gained at the Royal Academy and stuff like that.

Under my parliamentary hat, I shall ask the Minister, 'How many holders of Dramatic Diplomas at tertiary level currently reside in Wimpole Street?' and if the answer is 'One, in the maisonette at No. 22,' I shall have something to say about their promise of secrecy.

But while there was mild resentment (more like pique, really) by us Heads of Households at the number of questions, we professionals in whatever it is that we do were saddened at the things they might have asked and did not. There is so much that those who move around the kitchen tiles would like to know and would have found out, had they given us a dozen more spaces, like:

Do you eat tinned peas for choice?

Should Daddy's, HP, Flag and AI be taken into public ownership?

Put in order of importance: hot plate timing device, kebab skewer, larding needle, rotary spit, grapefruit knife, butter mould, meat thermometer, fondue set, waffle iron.

Do you own a pepper mill and does it work a) sometimes b) never? (Should there be any other answers, the country would like to hear from you.)

How many herb jars do you own?

How many herbs have you used in the last week/month/year?

Can you tell the difference between butter and margarine?

Do you own a blender—in which case do you buy caster sugar? Why?

How many cookery books do you own?

How many have you read?

How many do you still look at and which? (Now *there* is a question.)

Enough of this.

Seasons used to be all important when it came to food and until not-that-long-ago you could not buy fish in Birmingham. Sir Peter Parker, Sir Freddie Laker and their predecessors changed all that. Nevertheless, in May the asparagus in the shops will be English and Scottish and very much the better for that. Now, despite the delicacy of sparrowgrass, it is not a vegetable to eat neat and as there is a mystique about the difficulty of producing Hollandaise Sauce, I thought this might be a time, and place, to disabuse readers of that idea.

Let us begin with a butter sauce. Amazingly, this is the English name given to a white sauce in which you have dissolved butter—which has caused apoplexy among many French persons. The trouble about butter and hot food is that butter melts and the resultant yellow oiliness is of only small appeal to the aesthete. There is a way:

In a small saucepan bring three tablespoons of water to the boil and add six ounces of butter, cut into small cubes, three or four at a time, and add more cubes when these have melted. When the water/butter mixture rises in the pan (the way milk rises when it boils), pour the contents into a cold basin and whisk for fifteen seconds—or wildly agitate a fork if you have no whisk. The mixture tastes like butter, is butter—but looks like cream.

Now for real Hollandaise which needs a little more attention. You need the yolks of two eggs, six ounces of butter and a coffee-spoon of lemon juice. Salt and pepper is up to you. Heat is the secret and there is many a little lady who starts with all the right ingredients and whisks away at a cold basin engaged over simmering water until she (or the sauce) expires from terminal dandruff.

Put a pudding basin into the oven until good and hot. Cut one ounce of butter into slivers and put these into the hot basin. Add the lemon juice and two egg yolks, starting to beat the mixture as soon as you put in the egg—and you do this on the work surface or window-sill or wherever. Heat the remaining butter in a pan until it has melted, is hot but has not browned. Dribble the melted butter into the basin with your left hand as you whisk with your right—or ask the butler to pour the butter as the housemaid wields the whisk, if you are that sort of family.

The result, achieved in a matter of very few minutes, is hot, thick, delicious and avoids all those boring 'engagements of basin over simmering pans' that you read about in the cookery books that you bought thinking that they would actually teach you something.

There will come a time when you make Hollandaise so well and so quickly that you will look beyond the domestic asparagus season for things with which to eat the stuff; try artichokes, new potatoes, leeks, poached eggs, and quite especially boiled fish, though if you live on the seaward side of Birmingham, you will probably get it so freshly caught it will need no more than a thin application of lime juice.

CHAPTER TWO

Very well, bread

Bread is unique . . . for in the entire gastronomic range there is no other product that arouses the same fervours and passions.

Quite apart from the fact that you can usually tell the difference between a fish finger and a loaf, it should be remembered that no one, absolutely no one at all, makes fish fingers from a deep-seated urge to do so.

They do in the case of bread.

It is a therapy and a stand-by. In times of trouble people can be roughly divided between those who pray and those who bake, and both processes have been able to claim considerable success. Pregnant women take to it and chairmen of multi-national companies when life seems hard . . . for there is something atavistic, basic and satisfying in taking a few unlikely ingredients and transforming them into what, on the face of it, you would have no right to expect: a crusty, sweet-smelling, nutritious, compulsive feast—fashioned from the ground content of wheatseed, particles of fungi of *Saccharomyces* and water.

There are few recipes for bread that do not work, but I would advise anyone who considers embarking on a career of baking (something that is recommended *before* psycho-analysis or the even darker alternative of involvement with hygienically-wrapped, pre-sliced, steam-baked bread) to begin with a basic loaf.

Assemble a bag of flour, a packet of dried yeast, a small bottle of cooking oil, sugar and salt. You could also have a teacup, a large mixing bowl, some warm water and a baking tin which should be of the shape in which you want the loaf to end up—square, round, oblong or whatever.

Fill one cup (never mind what size cup as long as you go on using it and no other) with flour (any flour) and decant it into the basin through a sieve. Add the contents of the packet of dried yeast—half an ounce is the weight they tend to write on the outside—and a rounded teaspoon of sugar.

Now fill the cup to overflowing with warm water and pour this on to the slour/yeast in the basin, using a hand whisk to obtain a smooth creamy mixture which will begin to froth a bit as the yeast goes about its business. Let it stand for a couple of minutes as the bubbles rise.

Now add $2\frac{1}{2}$ more cups of sieved flour, a spoonful of salt and a dessert spoon of vegetable oil. Use a wooden spoon to roughly pull the mixture together and decant it on to a floured work surface for the kneading.

This is the good part. You start off with this sticky ball of flour and yeast and water—made less sticky by dusting with flour—and by punching it and picking it up and slamming it down and pushing the extremities into the middle and using your palms to try and push it into the work surface . . . you end up with a soft spongy slightly shiny ball of well-mixed dough. The process takes around three to five minutes.

Lightly grease a decent-sized pan such as will comfortably hold twice the amount of dough that you currently have, place the dough in this, cover with lid and keep in a warmish place for an hour and a half when it will have doubled in size . . . the warmer the place, the faster the 'rise', but there is no virtue at all in overdoing the heat.

When the dough has risen to twice its volume, turn it out on the re-floured work surface and punch it down again. Then put it into a properly greased baking tin in which it will assume its final shape in the oven and let it rise again . . . which will not take much more than half an hour.

Use the last twenty minutes of this time to pre-heat the oven to gas mark 8 (450°F) and bake the loaf for twenty minutes at that temperature; a further twenty-five minutes on mark 6 which is fifty degrees cooler.

Let it cool on a rack and eat it as soon as it is cool enough to touch. You may also try to let it cool completely—a good test of will-power, this—and if you are very successful, try writing to the Editor of the *Guinness Book of Records* telling him for how long you held out and seeing whether you may not have achieved some sort of 'first'.

When you have successfully achieved your first loaf the whole world of baking is your oyster. There are different kinds of flour which will make loaves darker or whiter, coarser or smoother.

You may use milk or watered milk instead of straight water.

Make fruit loaves with grated apples; or chips of green bananas or currants or chopped raisins mixed into the dough.

Use more salt in the dough *after* the yeast has begun to work (salt has a negative effect on yeast) or roll the finished dough ball in salt crystals, or cracked wheat.

Paint the outside with egg yolk or cream to get a shiny finish . . . or paint your name, or your loved one's favourite habits, on the loaf.

Experiment with black treacle or molasses to get marbled bread . . . the bread possibilities are endless . . . and when the dough has risen and been knocked down, try out different shapes: for instance, roll out the dough, cut it into three long strands and plait them.

Have a go with baking powder which will give you a lighter loaf. Try small bread rolls and long bread sticks.

Get into bread. Read bread books and bread pamphlets such as millers distribute with flour and for heaven's sake don't be afraid of telling people that it is you who bake and if the national loaf is going to get worse or more expensive, you might take it up as a business.

There is little in life more impressive than the secretary who recently countered my request to speak to her boss with the words: 'I am afraid I cannot disturb the Chairman. He is awaiting the second rising.'

The Crawfy syndrome is a journalistic malaise, to which weekly publications are more prone than dailies; in effect it inhibits comment lest this be overtaken by events . . . like the analytical discussion of Neville Chamberlain's Peace in Our Time announcement which appeared in the September 1939 issue of a monthly that went to the printers some months before it reached the bookstalls. ('Crawfy' was the Queen's nanny who wrote a glowing description of Her Majesty at Royal Ascot for a woman's magazine, in the year Royal Ascot was cancelled.)

As I write, *HMS Invincible* is steaming towards the Falklands; as you read this it may be steaming with greater or lesser urgency. It may even be steaming in a different direction.

Despite the syndrome, I shall write about the event: one of the main hold-ups to immediate movement of the Armada to the South Atlantic was caused by victualling. The Secretary of State did not give details, but when he explained that 'one cannot just send so many destroyers, corvettes, submarines, etc. to a destination 8,000 miles away', he meant that you had to think about food and drink.

The guns are ready, the decks clean; Véry-light pistols, cannon balls, and all the other items of sophisticated warfare can be assembled in a matter of hours . . . but the wherewithal for breakfast, dinner, lunch, and tea for so many thousand people, for a journey that might take a very long time, needs, as we say in politics, the most careful consideration.

Can you imagine the ignominy, the public loss of face, if the fleet had to turn back after three days at sea because they had forgotten to bring vanilla essence?

I know about these things: I once victualled a boat for a journey across the South Atlantic, and when we ran out of ground almonds on the ninth day out of Cape Town, things could have got very ugly.

I kept a notebook by my bedside table for two months before

the journey, would wake up in the middle of the night, put down 'birthday candles' and sink back into relieved sleep. The Navy must take it from me that Lists are essential. One of the other problems is that you have a captive audience; and pleasant as it is to know that none of your disenchanted clientèle can threaten to take their custom elsewhere, it is no fun having a crew that is unhappy about the victualling. It was here that I found involvement so useful.

I invented a baking process called Bread in the Round, which is like singing in the round in that it allows practitioners of limited ability to lend their talents to achieving something when all their instincts would have them sit around and achieve nothing. It is a co-operative activity, possibly making it eligible for EEC grants, and requires flexi-time work—just so long as the time is flexed apropos the work in hand.

Bread is a rewarding thing to make, and the stages of baking go well with the traditional naval watches. We were fifteen men on board the *Ocean Spirit*, and if the aircraft carrier *Invincible* wants to emulate our example, she will have to multiply. If *you* wish to do what we did, divide, unless you are numerous, or have a freezer.

The first stage is to dissolve the powdered yeast. For six loaves, I would leave out three packets of dried yeast (1½ozs), a large bowl and half a teacupful of sugar. Also a whisk. The instructions were to put yeast and sugar in the bowl, add two teacupsful of flour and six teacupsful of warm water. Then you just whisk and wait until the next watch takes over.

Instructions an hour or so later, when the sugar/flour/yeast/ water mixture was tacky and blended, were to add 7 cups of flour, half a cup of oil, quarter a cup of salt, blend all this to a mass with a wooden spoon, and then knead the mass while there was time from the raising and lowering of the spinnaker! (I am aware of the fact that aircraft carriers do not use spin-nakers; I expect they have similar time-consuming equipment.) At the end of the watch, they were instructed to leave the kneaded dough on an oiled tray, covered by a tarpaulin.

Three hours later, the third watch decanted the dough on to a flat surface, knocked it down (it had risen) and cut the dough into 6 loaf-shaped pieces which went into the greased bread-tins, which were filled to the half way mark, and the next watch—probably the ones who had started the whole shooting match, slept and come back—gave the knocked-down dough two hours to re-rise and then baked it in a medium-hot oven for 45 minutes per 2lb loaf.

We also made brown bread by adding gravy browning at the first stage; and garlic bread by forgetting to rinse out the bread-tins after cooking garlic stew in them the night before. I leave other variations to the imagination of the reader.

One of the chief advantages was that when the bread did not rise, or manifested some other sign of failure, *everyone* was to blame; so that the chef walked proud, when he might have been made to walk the plank.

If we are to believe that the sandwich owes its existence to the well advertised reluctance on the part of Lord Sandwich to have his card-games interrupted by meal-breaks—and that the nobleman's chef, unable for some reason to obtain tin-foil or plastic bags, put the Earl's sustenance between slices of bread thereby allowing the good man to shout 'Snap' throughout the night without collapsing of hunger—this clearly dates the advent of anchovy paste, cucumber spread and Primula cheese, none of which can conveniently be consumed *au naturel*.

(Why it took upward of 8,000 years from the discovery of bread to the realisation that you could slice it and put things on it and in it, is another matter and remains a mystery.)

However, it is since the episode of the crumbs on the green baize table that products ancillary to bread have come into their own, for prior to that the world was beset with ecological imbalance: the sea was rotten with sardines waiting for the invention of toast; baked beans grew apathetically on bushes and it was the peanut butter butty concept that gave the world Jimmy Carter who, without bread, would have remained good old Jimmy Who in the struggling hog-food and nut-oil business.

If you look with care at the industries that are almost totally dependent on the produce of others, it is sad to notice how rarely—other than via mergers and takeovers—they operate in unison. If I owned a mint farm I should send Christmas cards and Get Well messages to all sheep-farmers everywhere. Were my prosperity to stem from cranberries, my waking hours would be spent encouraging the turkey trade. I mention all this because I recently led a deputation of fruit growers to the Minister of State, Department of Agriculture, to acquaint him of the serious effects which the import of East European strawberry pulp was having on the British soft fruit industry . . . and one of his horticultural advisers explained that there was an established and accelerating decline in jam consumption.

That makes sense: the main users of jam are the institutions —works canteens, schools, prisons and hospitals, all in recession. Jam sauce went with roly poly and thanks to the jam manufacturers' failure to appreciate this, when roly poly went to the wall, jam suffered. What did not make sense was that bread was allowed to go into a steadily declining sales-curve without any sort of campaign mounted on its behalf by those industries dependent upon buoyant bread sales—like jammers.

A look at butter and margarine during this period is perplexing; the sales of both went up as the sale of bread went into a forty per cent overall decline; as a nation we were putting more fat on less bread, or perhaps more realistically, we were compensating for the loss of quality of the produce of the British Bakehouse. As both butter and margarine improved, bread was getting ever more boringly, predictably and massively standardised. Eighty per cent of our bread came from three, then two, giant firms that used computers and technology where once we had baked with hands and skill.

Gone were the crusty loaves because the shelf-life of a crust was unacceptable to supermarket philosophy. Gone were the oddly-shaped cottage loaves because they took up too much space on the delivery van and, as bread became poorer in quality and range, so was there an upsurge in the quality and the range of what was put on it and in it. Butter sales *up*. Premium margarine sales *up*. Meat paste *down*. Fish paste *down*. High class jams *up*. It is the bottom of the market jams, the Co-op and Hartleys and Robertsons and Chivers and chain stores' own-label jams which were acceptable with fresh crusty bread that simply will not do to take the boredom out of steam-baked, double wrapped pre-sliced standard loaves.

And while the Gollywog of yore pales and becomes redundant, Tiptree and Elsenham flourish. A new brand called Mrs Bridges, all sizzle and no steak as they say in the United States, appears at County Fairs and speciality shops in cunningly-shaped glass containers with olde worlde labels and a cover of gingham just as if Mrs Bridges of TV fame had torn a piece from her apron. Is Mrs Bridges' jam good, do I hear you ask? Good heavens; who would know that? It is a jam for giving rather than for eating.

English Provender of Aldreth is good. Nice, plain containers and pretty labels using sixteenth century calligraphy and interesting concepts like 'raspberry and kirsch' without any indication of the ratio in which the two named ingredients are to be found. Could it be the pork and grouse pâté syndrome?

'What proportion of grouse?' I asked, when I was offered a tasting.

'Fifty-fifty,' replied the manufacturer, and it was not till later that I discovered he meant fifty fat sows to fifty grouse.

To go back to jams, home-made jams are best. Like soups, the smaller the quantity you produce, the more accurately you can judge the cooking time, the flavour and the solidity of the end product. If you like liqueur in your jam, only in your own brand will you know how much was put in. At the time of year when plums at the roadside are selling for single figure pence per pound and homecoming holidaymakers are bringing home Spanish and Greek brandies that cost less than the same volume of double cream, get out some trusty cookery book and try your own plum jam. If it sets, so be it. If it fails to abandon its runny state, you call it a brandied plum preserve and serve it with cream, double cream if you are rich.

I was talking to a French civil servant about the lovely people of Martinique and he said, in Franglais, 'C'est tout la faute de votre bloody Capitaine Bleek.'

'Bleek?'

'Oui, bloody Capitaine Bleek of le bloody bateau *Bounty*. Lui et his bread-fruit.'

Truly the French blame us for much and nowhere do they blame us with more vehemence than in the field of cookbooks. La Madame Beeton est un huge joke on the far side of Calais. They do not understand Mrs David, do not bother to translate the excellent Margaret Costa, whose *Four Seasons Cookbook* is quite one of the best compilations on the market, and as they cannot pronounce 'Leith' they miss a bit there, too.

I re-read Beeton the other day—that is to say, I plunged into a 1963 version of *Everyday Cookery* written by one of her successors, in her style; as she and the boring M. Larousse write with all the flair and innovation shown by the authors of the classified telephone directory this gave no great pleasure, but one must bear in mind that both volumes are for looking things up in, rather than reading.

Opposite page 464 there was a picture of a table set for a grand tea, beneath which it advised you to study pages 506/8 to learn about cakes and page 502 for details of the sandwich loaf.

Le sandwich loaf is the sort of confection the French never ever give at le fif o'clock; in fact I cannot put my hand on my heart and remember when I last saw a sandwich loaf anywhere, so I paged on and found out.

You get this day-old loaf, wrote whoever it was who called himself Beeton in 1963, and take off the rinds and cut it into five slices, lengthwise. Then you spread slice number one with a mixture of ham and mayonnaise, the next slice with crushed hard-boiled egg, the next with sardine and the fourth with cream cheese. (You use the fifth slice to cover the cheese on the fourth.) Then you moisten some cream cheese with milk to make it more pliable and use green colouring because it has such a pretty effect and slap it around the confection; decorate the three sides of the loaf with slices of tomatoes and olives. If you do not need it you can wrap it in damp greaseproof paper, then in a cloth, and keep it in a refrigerator until you want it; this is their final jibe to the reader (though why you should

24

make the thing if you did not need it is beyond my comprehension).

You can just imagine the scene when the Dubois family call upon the Smiths. 'Bonjour, Monsieur and Madame Dubois. I have just the little delicacy you will enjoy straight from Madame Beeton,' says Lady S, and she goes to the refrigerator, opens the cloth and proceeds to pull damp greaseproof paper—and bits of tomato and olive that will stick to it—off the loaf.

How to get it on to the serving plate without leaving your fingerprints is not disclosed but I fancy a palette knife slipped under the wet base might do the trick, if there is any fight left in the bottom slice.

I much admire the mixture: matured sardine living it up above the old chopped egg, cream cheese at the top end of the loaf and then again outside it, admittedly with green colouring (optional) to charm the guest. Cutting the loaf is going to be fun, too; you have this light-green-coloured brick with bits of tomato and olive sticking to the tacky cheese, and a bread-knife is simply not the implement to dismember the confection into thin slices shown on the picture, for pressure will do no more than meld the top into the bottom and provide a multi-coloured pudding—a guillotine would be best.

But if you take all the advice and manage to make the loaf and get the slices on to a dish, the joy is going to come when your guests sit at the tea-table. On no account must you provide forks or napkins.

A tea-time buffet is something that not nearly enough is written about these days and if you ignore pages 502 and 506/8 you can do terribly well with an assortment of breads: brown, spiced, soda, ginger, currant, fruit etc.; serve best unsalted butter in a large slab at room temperature and a selection of good jams, honeys and lemon curd. Make scones and serve them warm and have lightly-beaten double cream which is a nice contrast in colour and texture to the strawberry preserve which you serve with it—and if you want to make sandwiches, then brown bread cucumber ones are best, thinly cut, and for heaven's sake do not garnish the outside.

Damp greaseproof, an olde granny trick, is a wondrous way

of preserving bread for a few hours just as long as you do not intend to eat the outside slice or any on to which the dampness of the paper has seeped. If you want to have the best of both worlds you could wrap your freshly-made, thinly-cut cucumber sandwiches in some slices of bread which you wrap in damp greaseproof. That should keep everyone happy, including the bakers.

Where Beeton is so useful is that reading her makes you remember; for instance that fruit salad is a great idea for a buffet tea. Stop there; put away the tin-openers, try a few Kiwi fruit peeled and sliced and mixed with an Ogen melon similarly cleaned up; add lemon syrup (sugar and water boiled together and lemon juice added when it cools); chill the fruit salad, and the Dubois family will go away protesting that *la cuisine anglaise* is vraiment too much. Vraiment. I mean really trop.

Passing through a doctor's waiting room the other day, I chanced upon a publication from which the honest well-fed face of Robert Carrier stared back, unequivocally. (I used to get Carrier and the Queen Mother confused, but finally sorted them out by recalling their respective talents in noblessing and obliging.) The magazine was one that recommended readers to buy vellum covers so that you could buy more Carrier magazines and build up a Carrier library, which must be very helpful to one and all, as the late Damon Runyon used to say.

On the ninth page (page 396 as they call it, so that you feel a shit for not having purchased the previous 43 editions), the great man gave a masterclass, which taught you to make something, I forget just what; it was memorable in that it allowed the author, who is an elegant writer, to go on at length about some process upon which cookery writers normally spend about ten words. 'Rub flour into butter,' we say, 'until the consistency resembles breadcrumbs.'

Carrier went on to describe the type of flour, the temperature of the butter and the size of the pieces thereof, the ideal shape of the bowl, the perfect position of the fingers, the texture of the

26

sieve through which you strain icing sugar and then strain it again, and the deeply satisfying feeling of—well, rightness would be the word, would it not?—of the breadcrumb-like substance which you need before you set out on the next little stage of the operation.

I want to write about Welsh Rarebit, which many cookery books would have you believe is melted cheese on toast; let me disabuse you of this over a few hundred words.

There is a school of thought that would have you buy the most expensive matured Farmhouse Cheddar—and while I am a great fan of Farmhouse cheeses, this sort of advice is similar to recommending that you use Louis Roederer Crystal Brut Champagne in Black Velvet Cocktails. You just go ahead and buy any Cheddar-like cheese: Cheshire, Leicester, Caerphilly will do well and if they are a bit stale, so much the better; well, cheaper.

Grate this on that part of the apparatus which gives you soft worms of cheese rather than the apertures that provide grains—and to six ounces of grated cheese you add one whole egg and one egg yolk, beaten together. You blend the egg and the cheese and now have an acceptable texture on which to work.

Add Dijon mustard and cayenne pepper and only *you* know in what quantities. A level dessertspoon of tomato purée is handy, especially if you used a chalky cheese and want people to think you bought red Cheshire especially for them. A shake of Worcestershire Sauce is good (were this not a masterclass, it would have been Worcester) and a teaspoon of grated onion gives you an even better reason for not buying expensive cheese. Pour in a table-spoonful of stout or brown ale just before the final mix, spread generously on freshly-made toast, placing the confection quite a long way beneath the source of the flame, which should be set around medium fierceness; that way the mixture is cooked thoroughly before the top becomes attractively speckled with evidence of heat. If it goes black and bursts into flames, you have not followed my instructions as carefully as I had hoped.

The size of toast is important; a whole slice of toast from a square loaf is too large for most people and demands too much cheese and is unsubtle. (Our national practice of serving things on toast actually came about by caterer's meanness; they used to serve grilled mushrooms and people complained about how few mushrooms they got. Bingo, said an inspired portion-control man. We will serve them on toast and then we can say, 'That's all the mushrooms we could get on that piece of toast.')

Remove the rind from a piece of freshly-grilled toast, cut it into fingers, aiming for one inch by four, and pile upon this the cheese mixture to a depth fractionally thicker than was the slice of bread.

In olden receipts for a Rabbitt, which is what they called rarebits, it was decreed that you should use toast soaked in wine, occasionally bread soaked in wine and toasted, and you will find this in the literature of English cookery throughout the eighteenth and nineteenth centuries. I spent an evening with bread and wine and, while I was at it, bread and beer, bread and rum, and bread and brandy. I used bread neat and toasted; I sprinkled it and dipped it and drowned it. I grilled it slowly and quickly and to each I added the cheese mixture and grilled as instructed.

Each result was a dead ringer for the soggy slice they slip under most savouries that we get in the House of Commons canteen.

I re-read my ancient cookery bookes: 'Soake in wine' stared at me from a dozen printed pages. Some urged me to pile on the cheese and let it bake in an oven, some to hold over it a salamander, which is a piece of red-hot radiating metal at the end of a wooden handle—a sort of grandfather of the modern grill. I baked and grilled the anointed soaked bread in various ovens for most periods of time in the calendar. Even when the bottom became crisp, the part between that and the cheese layer remained red sog—vineous blotting paper. I tried it with white wine: white sog. I grilled the moistened bread under fast and slow grills; the results were equally disgusting—for there is no way that soggy bread can be brought back to edible life other than as part of a forcemeat, pudding or dumpling.

(On the subject of dumplings I do wish they would come back into popular use. Perhaps we could try to get some upcoming twelvemonth designated The Year of the Dumpling and then Mrs Thatcher and the Chancellor could do something for them.)

'It is all a matter of linguistic continuity,' said the man from Reading University. The reason why we say 'er' or 'umm' (hardly anyone says both) also 'actually', 'obviously' 'basically' and 'y' know' is because we don't want the opposition to take over the conversational void caused by our inability to think of the next apposite remark.

Gastronomically, that is what crisps, peanuts, small hard green olives and Ritz biscuits are about: meaningless diversions that nevertheless occupy hand, glottis and toothpick. As the incisive speaker uses only words for which he has genuine need —see *Hansard* once the editors are done with it—so does the essential gourmet eschew the 'knowwhatImeans' from his diet. The professor of philology made much of the juxta-positioning of meaningless phrases: 'This is my cousin, y' know' is, for instance, quite different from 'This is my, y' know, cousin.'

And with food there is a substantial difference in when you indulge in pointless consumption. Eat a few peanuts before the soup and you glean general nods of affirmative indifference; grab a handful of them between meat and pudding and see what your hostess has to say about that.

The err-less, umm-less eater concentrates on atavism. Soup, meat, sweet, with not a trace of one in the other, like no soup in the meat, no sugar in anything but the pud. Pot roast is the dish for him. No element of 'See here, old chap, I mean to say, what?' about pot roast.

You get a 3lb piece of the very best topside and brush the outside with melted butter into which you have lavished salt and freshly-ground peppercorns. Put your heaviest saucepan— ideally one made of iron or aluminium—on to a high flame and when it begins to emit wisps of blue smoke from the base, you are ready for action. Put in the meat (which will sizzle mightily), seal it all around by the fierce heat of the pan and then turn down the flame somewhat, engage a well-fitting lid and allow twelve to twenty minutes per pound, turning the joint at half-time.

Extinguish the source of heat at the appropriate time and leave for 10 to 15 minutes to produce its own liquor, with which you anoint the slices you carve.

As an accompaniment to it, spinach springs to mind as being more suitable than a purée of celeriac and artichoke hearts stuffed into a tomato, garnished with grated cheese and glazed beneath the grill, which is an 'asamatteroffact' kind of dish.

I often wonder about bread and butter with a meal; it is a commodity in which absolutely everyone seems to be interested —with the exception of the diner. The crockery trade, cutlery merchants, bakers, flour millers and the whole dairy industry depend on you to make inroads into what they put upon your side-plate.

There was a time when hoteliers had a vested interest in having you eat bread. In the days of the three-course *table d'hôte*, they reckoned that the more bread and butter they could shovel into you at the start of a meal, the smaller the amount of expensive meat and sherry trifle you would need at the end. *Table d'hôte* went the way of snoek; bread stayed. And whereas sensible restaurateurs try to confine your starch and fat intake so that you will have a moneymaking appetite for smoked salmon, partridge, and raspberries, there are others who give you the gastronomic equivalent of a chronic stammer: rolls, breadsticks, radishes, sticks of celery, herb butter, anchovy butter, cucumber, carrot.

Petits fours were once a sign of a grand, rather than an ordinary meal. Sugar-based hiccups, they were served on gold or silver plate to divert the consumer while the port wended its inevitable clockwise course.

Now everyone is doing it. Egg and chips and After Eight mints. Hamburgers followed by a selection of Smarties and Jellybabies. The principal idea is to confuse; comes the bill—a modest charge for food bloated by cover and coffee and service and VAT. Just as you are about to make a fuss you remember the 'free' piece of fudge and the candied grape and leave an extra five per cent.

30

Petits fours are the final verbal affectation. The caterer's way, if you like, of, sort of, in a manner of speaking . . . conning you; see what I mean?

CHAPTER THREE

Commoners and kings

In the final analysis ... when the blame comes to be apportioned ... will it be the wet-nurses, the nannies or the educationalists who must take the rap for our dishonesty? Goodness knows, we did not set out in life to be deceitful.

It sort of crept up on us at the instigation of our mentors: 'Promise to be a good boy, and I will bring you back a baby brother or sister from the hospital,' (as if there was a choice).

Promise to go to sleep?

Promise to eat your tapioca pudding?

Promise to wash behind your ears?

Childhood was replete with promises, paid for by promissory notes with only an occasional snatch of reality in the form of small, crisp pieces of green or brown paper bearing the legend 'I promise to pay on demand ...' and signed by one K. O. Peppiatt, Cashier of the Bank of England, the lord high promiser.

By the time I joined the Scouts, promissory words poured from my lips like the Wordsworth Sonnet which I had been forced to commit to memory in detention ('earthasnotanything-toshowmorfair, dulwoodebeofsoloocudpasby' etc).

The ten sub-sections of the Scout Law fortunately escape me

at this moment, though I recall that one of the promises I made was to 'smile and whistle under all difficulties'. In a life beset with hardship I am remembered (if I am remembered at all) for my steadfast reluctance to smile, coupled with a total inability to whistle. Readers will be interested to learn that I rose nevertheless to become Deputy Leader of the Peewit Patrol, my first executive appointment.

Still wearing that passé felt hat of Lord Baden-Powell's I also promised to help other people at all times; a promise manifested on wet Saturday afternoons in easing elderly ladies across St John's Wood Road, where a fellow-scout, an up-and-coming chap in the Curlews, helped them back whence they had come.

That job well done, we would repair to the Black and White Milk Bar (not realising in those green and salad days of youth that this was probably the Nuremberg, the Worms, the very foundation stone of racialism) and drink a daring 'shake'; the ambition at the time was to engage the serving lady in conversation so that the mixture of milk and ice-cream and chocolate had an extra moment or two of froth-producing agitation in the machine. 'You're trying to make me forget the machine is on,' she would accuse.

'No we didn't,' we said. 'Promise.'

Over the next decade I made a number of fleeting promises to headmasters, army officers and employers. A serious promise to a lady called June Flewett about loving, honouring and obeying (the third of these promises was broken at 8.45 p.m. on our wedding day by me; at 8.46 p.m. by her).

But the past is behind us (June Flewett is not; she is downstairs watching television); a past punctuated by the tiny barbs of broken promises none of which seemed to do me any more harm than that hollow phrase of K. O. Peppiatt's, the great redeemer.

Currently the path I pursue is that ultimate game of promises: politics. 'Vote for me and you shall have houses and greater pensions. More oil will flow more profitably as a direct result of the cross made against my name and wide arterial roads will be built without ecological detriment; buses will run in all directions; trains will be frequent and punctual, employment office staff efficient and helpful, and doctors shall insist on making house calls.

'Of course it is true; it is all in our manifesto called *Promise for the Future*.' The phrases are there for all to read, provided you enter the room marked 'meeting this day' or open the 'Election Communication' envelope.

For myself I found some time ago that the best political promises are those of doom. 'Mark my words' you will hear me shout from the steps of the town hall on selected autumn Saturdays—'there will be drought and famine in this land of ours. Unless strong and immediate action is taken today, blood will run in the gutters, the young will stagger illiterate through a life punctuated by dole queues, soup kitchens and charity hand-outs. The pound will achieve parity with the lira, while Arabs walk the streets knocking British people off the pavements.'

The appeal of such promises is that if they materialise, your spring Saturdays are taken up saying, 'I told you so.' However, in the unlikely event of things getting better there is no more attractive theme for a speech than to say, 'Ladies and gentlemen. It was I, speaking from the steps of this very town hall, a few short months ago, who warned the government of impending doom. But for my hard-hitting words, blood would have run in the gutters, etc. . . .'

One of my early introductions to the ways of politicians occurred when I spent a weekend with a Tory ex-Minister in Suffolk. On the Saturday morning he took his house party on a drinks outing and on the way to the first pub he stopped at three shops, at each of which he bought half a pound of butter.

Noticing my raised eyebrows after the third halt, he explained that in his constituency the people liked to feel that the MP was 'around'; by the time we got back he had purchased a further two pounds of sugar, a tin of drinking chocolate and shown us a total of four public houses.

'To stay in one pub, or make purchases in depth at one shop,' he proclaimed, 'is the height of political ineptitude.'

I was reminded of this at the Hillhead by-election when a three-figure gaggle of Alliance workers fanned into the district for the greater glory of Mr Jenkins. When the time came to take coffee there were some who patronised the good ladies who served at the HQ coffee bar; others made for the nearby café.

'No, no,' said I, and drew up a plan of campaign as a result of which much shoe leather was used but the café owners of Partick and Hillhead West became tremendous SDP/Liberal supporters. One way to a café proprietor's vote is through his cash-till.

I do not know what it is about politicians and ham, but there is in the minds of most people some deep conviction that it would be wrong to give politicos any other fare. As Nietzsche enjoined readers to go to a woman with a whip, so does the world at large go to an MP with a slice of ham.

'I am calling on behalf of the local candidate.'

'Come in and have a ham sandwich.'

'May I come to your house and change between a meeting and a dinner?'

'A ham salad will be waiting.'

When they draw up the plan for a country visit, I always note on my timetable the frequent 'stop for refreshment'; on a good day, by which I suppose I mean a bad day, I am confronted by a minimum of one and a half pounds of sliced ham— all of which has been especially and thoughtfully purchased by supporters who know that an MP's visit equals ham.

How long must I wait before an MP's visit equals a Marks and Spencer pork pie?

The City of Ely used to make Freemen—an uplifting annual ceremony as a result of which those who had been honoured were allowed forever after to parade through the streets with their bayonets fixed; also to enjoy some other rich pickings. Ely lost its right to create Freemen after the re-organisation of local government (though we made a few before we realised we had been deprived of the legal machinery); I should like to get an honour for Marks and Spencer, such as the George

Cross awarded to Malta. M and S has not just done a great job providing pants and socks for one and all; they now have what is arguably the best food department of any chain store and caterers would be wise to look at some of these lines before they commit their own in-house gorillas to trying to make a go of it with pot or pan.

For a buffet luncheon the stores have what I consider to be the best pork pies on the market: six decent portions at 85p with a latticed top of crisp and succulent pie crust. Scotch eggs come in half-dozen packs and the centre is of chopped hard-boiled egg, which is an interesting departure from the norm, and goes well with apricot chutney. They sell roast chickens in as many flavours as potato crisp manufacturers now sell crisps: Tandoori, bacon, herb, paprika and more, and the range of bread is wide and appetising and, as I must have said before, there is hardly a bread which does not become delicious when splashed with water and given seven minutes in the top of a medium oven.

M and S food department salads are excellent; cakes and puddings very good indeed; fruit expensive but reliable; cheese enterprising and includes a 'cheese-plate', which gives you at a small cost a selection of half a dozen cheeses such as you might grab from a restaurant cheese trolley when the waiter is looking elsewhere.

For the host who hates cooking, the party-giver who prefers to spend the early evening out of the kitchen or the family upon whom some large group descends without notice—let alone the restaurateur whose chef walks out—there is much to command attention.

The PR man for the firm said Newcastle is the best store.

My favourite encounter at Hillhead came via a lady television reporter who approached me with a microphone, camera hovering behind, in SDP headquarters, and said: 'Did you know that your Edinburgh HQ has been bombed?'

'I do not have an Edinburgh HQ,' I said.

'Are you taking this seriously?' she asked.

As Eric Morecambe used to say, 'There's no answer to that,'

so I asked her if she would like a ham sandwich. I had four in my outside jacket pocket.

Let me add as a postscript to my enthusiasm for shop-bought, ready-cooked food, that freshness, which is such an enviable ingredient of home cookery, can be simulated by the addition of the odd fresh adjunct like herbs or lemon juice.

Sandwiches made with not tremendously fresh bread and OK-meat take on a new dimension of desirability when the slices are spread with a mix made of half a pound of butter, a teaspoon of lemon juice, a coffee-spoon of mustard, and some chopped parsley. There is hardly a shop-bought fruit pie that does not become a gourmet dish when it is heated and has added to it fresh cream whipped with a spoonful of liqueur or grated lemon peel, and sugar if you are a child or teetotal. Try it next time you see an apple pie.

I am bemused by date-stamps. Most of the time you buy food and there is no indication of when it is too early or too late to eat what you purchase. But now and then there is a printed message: 'SELL BY NOV 24TH,' states a tub of margarine I came across the other day. Not BUY BY or USE BY which would make sense. Just SELL BY presumably because it will start to do things in the shop which they don't mind it doing out of the shop, like explode or melt or just smell worse then, than it does now.

Come to think of it, they don't tell you when it is too early, or DON'T SELL BEFORE as they might put it. Which is wrong. Wines ought to have labels warning consumers of infanticide in respect of say, 1979 clarets. Cheeses should have two notices: 'Don't sell before. Don't eat after.' That will save consumers from the evils of the unripe as well as the menace of the ammoniac.

At Safeway in the Kings Road, Chelsea (and I dare say in Pontefract and Tunbridge Wells, too, but I don't shop there), they have a special shelf upon which items are marked REDUCED, because they are within shouting distance of the SELL BY date. Cheeses are an excellent buy from that shelf . . . provided they are for dinner that night. Cream is a rotten buy, because unlike the olden days when cream was natural and went gently and acceptably sour, there is now so much chemical preservative and fixative and additive in cream that the stuff goes bitter and acid as soon as it ceases to be edible.

Statisticians who daily delight us with their findings about the hours we spend doing what ('Politicians spend an average of 17 minutes a week talking to their wives'), have not, to my knowledge, pontificated upon how much time we spend trying to call back to life things which are best left for dead. Granny told us about lamb cutlets: if they are off, she said, wipe them with a cloth soaked in vinegar. This is an absolutely super idea and should be practised by anyone who wants to eat a lamb cutlet which is not only off but manifests a patina of vinegar to boot. I have a Victorian Household Manual which advises readers to rub the inside of fish with salt, if it should be stale. That doesn't work either, for the fact is that when food is 'off' you may scrub and soak and salt and vinegar and marinate and flare in alcohol . . . if it was off before, it remains off.

During the war they used to curry stuff that was off and there are many people of my age and older who don't eat curry because they remember. The first time I ate proper curry I became retrospectively furious about all those abominations I had eaten thinking that that was what curry was about.

There is no sound reason for things to be 'off' in this day and age. Refrigeration, deep freezing, salting, marinating, jellying, even potting in clarified butter, all manage to keep the bacteria at bay. Marinating is best for fish and flesh.

The straight man's marinade is three measures of red wine to one of oil, to which you add of spices and herbs whatever will complement the object of your marination, bearing in mind that the marinade provides the base for the sauce.

For a leg of lamb purchased in a street market on a Saturday for consumption a week later, add to the wine and the oil some thinly sliced cloves of garlic, and sprigs of rosemary and coriander. No more. The idiots who throw on handfuls of oregano, ladles of Dijon mustard, spoonfuls of black treacle and smatterings of pounded mace and crushed ginger, get very little return for their investment.

38

For a delicate marinade for fish, say a 3 lb salmon trout, take a sherry glass of sunflower oil and three of dry white wine. Add some sprigs of fennel and a dozen peppercorns, roughly crushed. Cut off the head and tail of the fish and fillet the beast, because it is a great waste marinating a head and tail and bits of skin and bone.

If you want to keep soup (and there is a school of thought, to which my wife subscribes, which would have you boil it up twice daily) gelatin is a better idea. While the soup remains edible, it will stay in jellied form. When the jelly melts and bubbles rise to the top, you throw the soup away and if you think: I'll just boil it up and see, don't. Save the gas.

If unfermented cheese goes very stale, you can still use it for grating and putting into sauces and over soups. If fermented or blue cheese goes bad, that is it . . . and 'blue cheese dressing' for salads is not, honestly not, a good way of using up last month's Gorgonzola.

Old fruit can be used in sauces. Mouldy fruit cannot and old fat cannot be used in anything or for anything except feeding birds or as furniture polish, if you don't mind eating off a rancid dining table.

If I did not think that we already had far too many laws, I would suggest that compulsory labelling, both of origin and date of manufacture, should become mandatory. Damn it, we already do this with people: do not use sexually before the age of 16; do not use electorally before 18; and, at the other end of the scale, do not employ after the date of 60 or 65.

Quite apart from bad food, there is much that is wrong with the world.

I write—and therefore you read—this article because of that great and good and much understood man Angus Maude, Knight Bachelor—who would now be a Life Peer or possibly a Duke were it not for Mrs Thatcher's continuing reluctance to test her popularity in a by-election.

'What can you do,' he asked me (courteously pointing his smouldering cigarette in the direction of a rubber plant) 'about lettuce leaves? And cucumbers,' he added, 'also wedges of tired tomato? Why do they have to be draped across every plate bearing starters and why do I, who love potted shrimps above all things, have to winkle out my crustaceans from the folds of wilting greenery?'

I suggested that he table an Early Day Motion to the effect; advised him on reflection to propose an Anti-Garnish Bill under the Ten Minute Rule procedure and finally agreed to raise the matter in this column.

The reason for excesses of edible trappings is quite clear to us in the profession: it fills up the plate. It deludes you, the customer, into thinking that you are getting more of a deal than is actually being provided. A one and a half ounce sliver of terrine of duck riding an otherwise untenanted plate at an asking price of £3.25 smacks of daylight robbery. A similar slice, balanced upon a piece of lettuce, with two segments of tomato crouching alongside, all attended by a curlicue of cucumber sporting an application of mustard and cress, increases the food cost by hardly any money at all and makes you feel infinitely better. That's why.

Give a man a dozen peeled prawns in a wine glass topped with mayonnaise that has been spiked with tomato ketchup and Worcestershire sauce—and the chances are that he will zip a calculator from his jacket pocket, divide the price of the prawn cocktail by twelve and decide to take his trade elsewhere.

But confuse him by arranging the prawns among a welter of plucked escarole, frost the glass and thread a thin slice of lemon in and out of the rim, before anointing it with a sprig of borage, serve sauce apart, and the poor sod will look no further than your welcoming door. Now that the Chairman of the House of Commons Catering Committee has ordained that the French language be banished from the bill of fare (so that we are currently served egg and butter sauce when we used to get Hollandaise) it is perhaps time to consider the introduction of a whole new, far-reaching, honest approach to fleecing the restaurant customer.

Recent surveys have shown that no one much cares for bits of lettuce, let alone mustard and cress. I think I can state with some authority that if mustard and cress disappeared from the face of the earth, there would be limited wailing, hardly any gnashing of teeth and regret only from caterers who depend on something to disguise the fact that their sandwiches are curling at the edges, or the hard-boiled eggs have become discoloured.

Let them use parsley or provide blindfolds.

The French concept of *nouvelle cuisine* is based on serving ingredients as God might have done had he had the money—certainly the way health resort dieticians recommend—so perhaps the time has come for our side of the Channel to embrace a new deal which could, in time, come to be known as The New Deal. For the initial breaking-in period we might ban wafers with ice cream, cherries from drinks, pasta from soups, especially minestrone, and parsley and lettuce leaves from absolutely everything except parsley sauce and lettuce salad.

Let us run that up the flagpole and see who salutes it, as the Madison Avenue executives so picturesquely put it. If all is well after a month, I suggest we bring in the Grilled Tomatoes And Coolish Flabby Mushrooms As Accompaniments To Main Dishes Banning Order and follow that up with a Prohibition of Lemon Slices Bill. I believe that if food needs lemon, lemon should be provided in halves, proper wedges or possibly a small jug of freshly squeezed juice.

Sitting in the Lone Star Café one evening—this is situated on the corner of Harrington Gardens and Gloucester Road in South-west London—I chanced to overhear the girl at the next table disclose to her girl-friend that, 'I might be married to Dave but he's a bleeding waste of space.' I was eating a perfectly acceptable dish of blueberry ice-cream at the time but the statement from Mrs Dave, or possibly Lady Dave, made me appreciate it infinitely more, which goes to prove that it is not just the food but the overall atmosphere that determines enjoyment.

While the Palace of Westminster is very strong on pomp, it only gets about three out of ten for atmosphere and though the new all-English language bill of fare redresses the disgraceful purchase of German china in 1975, it does not do a lot for what the French used to call ambiance.

Had the Chairman of the Catering Committee been wise (and why should he bother; there is not a hope in hell of this lot giving him a life peerage) he might have taken steps to improve the food by going to the chef and suggesting ways to make things better. To go to the printer and determine how things might appear to be different manifests a negation of catering skills.

Such an exercise is best left to skilled public relations men who would have seen to it that we, who take the odd meal break from ruling the land, are spared the indignity of having to ask a Spanish waiter what 'male hen at the wine' used to be called in olden days . . . like last month.

You will probably know that it was I who opened the School Fête at Stuntney in July 1981; browsing among the junk stall I chanced upon a manual by 'A Victorian Housewife' in which the middle-class author provided for her readers some rather suspect philosophy in respect of the sort of occasions that will keep confronting the average woman. Such as : THE LOCAL MP COMES TO LUNCHEON BEFORE AN ENGAGEMENT. This is clearly written with something like the fête at Stuntney in mind; the advice is, frankly, disastrous.

'Provide for him a comfortable room in which he can rest. Leave him on his own with a bottle of whisky and a syphon of soda,' is how it begins. Victorian Housewife then, at some length and to my mind quite unnecessarily, instructs her readers on the preparation of a light meal comprising beef consommé, lamb chops, Stilton cheese and Bath Oliver biscuits. This is followed by good advice about presenting the children and decorating the table.

Imagine the scene: the MP has arrived, been conducted to his comfortable room and his whisky and the little woman gives a last touch to the cutlet frills while her husband decants the claret. The maid is sent to summon the Honourable Gentleman to the withdrawing room, at his leisure, and the children are lined up in order of seniority.

The well-ordered reception is startled by a scream; the

white-faced maid is seen racing down the corridor, pursued by a lurching red-eyed Member shouting reassuring obscenities. I mean, what the hell does Victorian Housewife expect?

What is now needed is not nourishing broth but a cold bath and much hot coffee. She mentions none of this. Someone will have to negotiate with the maid, say a month's salary and a veiled threat if she doesn't keep her mouth shut; this also is omitted from the manual and there is no advice on the message to the vicar—'Owing to a political crisis, unforeseen circumstances prevent the appearance of the guest of honour. Perhaps the Dean would very kindly agree to step in . . .'

I do not wish to register a serious complaint about a book which cost 5p, but nothing she writes would make me purchase sister volumes. Let us reassess the situation: given the *dramatis personae* of hosts, guest, maid, luncheon and whisky, the ideal solution is for Housewife to drink the Scotch, MP to cook the meal and Maid to take the children to a Chinese take-away.

Alternatively, show the MP to a comfortable room in which he can be alone with the sozzled maid, who will await him with what is left of the liquor. After a reasonable time, the hosts can bring them luncheon in bed. I suppose the real mistake was to ask the MP to luncheon in the first place. (On reflection, what was MP doing in his constituency? Or was there an election pending? If this were the case, MP would have been wiser to go to the local hostelry where they do like to see their parliamentary representative behaving as do the gentlemen at Westminster.)

What the tome does not mention is that one of the very hardest things to do is to entertain out of your social or economic station. The fact is that your silver, china and glass were bought with your sort of budget in mind, and whatever the budget, Lobster Thermidor on repro-willow pattern plates is as unacceptable as is a cheeseburger on Spode. A Woolworth tumbler in no way affects the taste of a fine claret, but it does deprive it of most of its glamour and all of the enjoyment that you had a right to expect. Limeade in Waterford crystal is just silly. I do not want at this point to rehearse the gastro-procedure of having the Wales's to dinner in your council house, other

43

than to say that they would have been unlikely to have accepted your invitation were they not prepared to accept your fare.

What I will discuss, briefly, is changing the nature of an occasion at short notice, which too many people think can be achieved by the random addition of cream or last-minute application of slivered truffle on the one end of the scale, mounds of chips and a lake of ketchup on the other.

My motto has always been, 'When in doubt, make them drunk.'

Failing that, an emergency larder of carefully collected delicacies is the best answer.

However humdrum the intended collation, croissants from the deep freeze, warmed in an oven and served with good butter, make it better. Few main dishes are not improved by a selection of interesting mustards, pickles, chutneys, and relishes.

Tinned soups, like mulligatawny and vichyssoise, mixed and warmed and anointed with a teaspoonful each of cream and sherry per bowl, make your guests hail you as a latterday Escoffier.

Bring back crystallised fruit from foreign holidays, kumquats from Corfu, plums in black chocolate from Yugoslavia, Hopjes from Holland, and if you went to Majorca, return with almonds. Take six ounces and place them in a bowl. Cover with boiling water and after one minute, pinch off the skins, mix with half an ounce of melted butter and a salt-spoon of salt and bake on an oven sheet in a slow oven (mark 3 is about right, 325°F if you are on electricity) and twenty minutes later they will be golden and crisp and buttery and salty and make your guests feel that the cottage pie is actually exactly what they wanted.

Among recent cuttings came information that some worthy charitable society, to whom I had sent a recipe for bread and butter pudding for inclusion in their *Celebrity Cookbook*, had received the self-same receipt from HRH Prince Charles.

This clearly put the charity into something of a dilemma: do they print his or mine? Do they go for snobbery or professionalism? His name on the jacket will ensure sales; mine will (or may) create goodwill in that readers will follow the instructions with confidence. He is far better known than I am as a prince. I am better known than he as a cook—in fact until I read his (my) recipe, I did not know that he cooked.

I telephoned the Press Office at Buckingham Palace; they did not know he cooked, if 'not to the best of my knowledge he doesn't' means what I take it to mean. I wish celebrity cookbooks would concentrate on what famous people eat, which is of a consuming interest, and ignore how he or she may or may not prepare a dish which is irrelevant and probably misleading. Anyway, should you come across a bread and butter pudding by Prince Charles, do try it.

There used to be a lady who sold marvellously esoteric and out of print cookery books under the name of Abigail; she sold out to Piccadilly Rare Books Ltd. who still send me their catalogues which now include such down-to-earth publications as *Delia Smith's Cookery Course* (1981), corners bumped, some foxing otherwise in good condition.

Browsing through the catalogue, I found: 68 *Docking* (Betty) compiler. Delectable Dishes. Cookery Recipes contributed by the Brighton and Hove housewives with a short supplement on Delectable Drinks prescribed by Brighton and Hove husbands. Slim royal 8vo; 72 pages, advertisements throughout, decorated paper covers, a bit bumped but in good condition. Southern Printing Co. (Brighton) nd. c. 1960. Recipes include: Traffic lights, Sussex Plum Heavies, Apple Dappy, Mayonnaise (uses more water than oil).

It was the 'more water than oil' bit that made me think. Oil thickens and water thins. More water than oil means more thin than thick. Mayonnaise is thick. Do I pay the asking price of £2 to find out that it will not be mayonnaise? Did a lot of people in 1960, sorry, c. 1960, pay a shilling to learn that secret? I doubt it, else we cookery writers (Prince Charles, Elizabeth David and I) would have heard about it and passed it on to our readers.

We must accept that Celebrity Cookbooks, Housewives' Cookbooks, Hollywood Stars Cookbooks *et al* are of considerable historic and sociological interest but should not be confused

45

with cookbooks written by people who put their names and reputations (as cooks) on the line.

Piccadilly Rare Books sell *The First Ladies' Cookbook*—favourite recipes of all the Presidents of the United States—'Recipes include Chess Cakes, Tyler Pudding, Maryland Caramel Potatoes etc.' Not a sign of the 10 Downing Street companion volume, possibly because the Civil Service provides the same cook irrespective of the identity of the incumbent of the property. The Alliance will soon change that.

I can imagine all sorts of people who would like to know that Hoover ate brownies, Eisenhower plumped for black pudding, Roosevelt adored semolina—Franklin D. that is. Theodore was a meat and potatoes man, but to follow the recipes when you could follow those of Julia Child is not wise.

Lot 84 among Piccadilly Rare Books is *From Sturbridge Kitchens* collected by the Evening Women's Club, Sturbridge Federated Church, Sturbridge, Massachusetts. This volume includes red pepper jam (1lb Victoria plum to 1 bottle Tabasco?) and 'at least 12 uses for a tin of tomato soup'. It really is much more fun reading the catalogue than the book. Let us try and work out the twelve uses.

Heating in the oven, wrapping in a flannel vest and using as a hot water bottle is obviously one. Throwing at attackers could be another, especially for evening women. Rolling small pieces of pastry, unless the tin is large in which case the size of the pastry could be bigger. Dropping it from a great height on to the back of a cake tin to loosen the pastry, juggling, cracking cob-nuts, using the label to test eye-sight, practising tying bow ties and basic knots around it, using it as a target for fire-arms, killing spiders, trapping ants, and balancing it on your head for posture classes is a round dozen. I wonder how many I got right, and I just hope they did not suggest opening it and eating the contents. I do not have to buy rare books for that sort of information.

Forget about *The South American Gentleman's Companion*. Volume One is an exotic cookbook (or up and down the Andes with knife, fork and spoon), Two an exotic drink book (or up and down the Andes with jigger, beaker and flask). I have been to the Andes and found no gentlemen; only a surfeit of chilli peppers. Among the lower price range—£1.50 to be precise—is *Personal Recipes* published by the East Kent Federation of Women's Institutes in the vintage year of c. 1960 and including such East Kent favourites as sheep's head broth, pilaf of pig's offal and curried tripe. I must go to East Kent more often. I had no idea they were so, what shall we say, *bas cuisine*.

If you bear in mind that Piccadilly lists one nineteenth- and one eighteenth-century book; that the former sells at £40, the latter at £75, you would be foolish not to dig a hole in your garden and fill it with all the cheap speciality books you can find. Wrap the books tightly in cling-film, then in aluminium foil and finally in a heavy polythene sack. This will save your heirs a great deal of money when it comes to christening presents for their great-grandchildren. 'Oick zzzmk poww,' they will proclaim, taken they are old enough. 1982 was a great year. Especially C. 1982.

Turning the pages of an old book by Marcel Boulestin (a well-known pre-war Frenchman who later became Philip Harben) I chanced upon a recipe for *tourin aux tomates*. It is a boring little soup achieved by frying eight slices of tomato and one chopped onion in 1½ ounces of pork fat. Add 1½ pints of water, some salt, much pepper and after simmering until the tomatoes are well cooked, pass through a sieve and add vermicelli to the broth which should cook for another six minutes. 'Even now in all the Perigord,' continues the scribe, 'this soup is offered to husband and wife on the wedding night. A large tureen is brought to them in great state by the neighbouring peasants, usually a few hours after the bride and groom have retired. They eat it in bed. The guests watch them and finish the rest. It seems more sensible than many old customs, such as throwing rice (un-cooked) at them in the street.'

Now I have in my time written about matters culinary and gastronomic; I have produced recipes, both literarily and actually, for banquets and picnics, luncheons and high teas, celebrations and revolutions; but it has never occurred to me to recommend the fare that should be consumed by a bride and groom a few hours after they have retired on their wedding night, let alone suggest what they might share with the local peasantry. Nevertheless I am convinced I could do better than clear tomato soup.

Imagine the scene: the couple are wed, the reception is over, the cake cut, the speeches made and the principals of this event have finally, self-consciously, retired to bed.

We now come to 'some hours later'. What are they going to need? I can put up a lukewarm argument for oxygen, Band-Aid, tetanus injections, a sex manual, even a book on do-it-yourself divorce. I simply do not accept that the right answer is tomato soup, 'brought to them in a large tureen in great state', though I too would be in something of a state to be thus confronted after the first flush of nuptial activity.

Under such circumstances my first choice would be to be left alone, which is why sensible honeymoon couples lock the bedroom door. As it is not within my remit to discuss solitude or security, I shall desist from further philosophy and concentrate upon food. And as Their Royal Highnesses may have wondered how they should have spent the time 'some hours after retiring on their wedding night', I shall write with them in mind: a menu for around 4 a.m. on July 30th, 1981. For a start, chocolate flake and cheese straws are out. The night is young and what is consumed must be capable of reaching the inner man and woman without the ensuing discomfort of crumbs. Soup with noodles is a rotten idea. Indeed, there is a better argument for Rice Krispies; these, at least, make some sort of accompanying noise, which could be useful—also, Rice Krispies are health-giving, sustaining, easily digestible, etc.

M. Boulestin did not state in his sketched account quite what it was that the wedding guests would have in mind when barging in on the happy couple but I presume that the idea is to see that all had gone well and to celebrate an interim state in the cementation of a relationship—the way American race-track commentators call the time at the two furlong post. Back to food.

Truffles in puff-pastry cases would be useful—delicious, rare and expensive; but puff-pastry crumbles and we did decide that nothing should disturb the smoothness of the sheets let alone the romance. I think the answer lies in the category of 'sweet or savoury'. A soufflé of wild strawberries, redolent of *eau de vie de framboise*, surrounded by crystallised ginger set in bitter chocolate, might suit, though if there are a lot of local peasants and, I presume, the intruding party would be joined by BBC, ITV and the gossip columnists, it might be advisable to have something with more longevity than a souflé; say, a fondu. Now that really is a very good idea—especially if they have a four-poster bed and you can hang the fondu pot from one of the crossplanks and use the drapes to wipe your hands.

You take equal quantities of Emmenthaler and Cheddar cheese, cut this into small pieces, melt it in just enough kirsch to turn the mass into a thick, smooth, heavy-porridge consistency over a low flame and spike with cayenne pepper. Provide snippets of fresh bread, which you dip into the fondu and unlike soup, which makes you sit in one place and slurp, fondu allows you to move around and get the best possible view of what is going on, possibly even evidence of what has been going on, which would be of especial benefit to the William Hickeys on this occasion.

There is another sort of fondu, known as 'Bourguignon', but I doubt whether the Royal couple would be up to it. The fondu pot is filled with boiling oil and the guests are given slivers of raw meat which they fry and then dip into selected accompanying relishes before consumption. It is a dish that will please all non-vegetarians because this is a many-splendoured thing. You can over- or under-cook the meat and dip into anything from chopped sweet gherkins to grated horseradish, via a tomato and garlic paste, tarragon mayonnaise, or anchovy sauce.

But do try to remember, Your Highness, that the oil has to be kept over a consistently high flame and that silk is highly flammable.

The old woman who lived in a shoe may not have been very

bright about birth control or environmental problems but she knew a thing or two when it came to catering and discipline.

You will recall that after outlining her whereabouts and predicament the author continues:

She gave them some broth without any bread
She whipped them all soundly and put them to bed.

I approve more of the sentiments of the first of these two lines than of the second, though in 1784, when Gammer Gurton's *Garland* was published, a light evening meal for the young coupled with a modicum of healthy exercise for grown-ups was probably standard practice. (One cannot help noticing the dearth of information that is available about 'the woman's' husband other than the implication that he was a pacifist and fertile with it.)

Broth has been with us since the beginning of gastronomic man, whose existence began twenty-five minutes after primitive man's discovery of fire and saucepan. The sequence can be readily imagined: man was thirsty and drank. In winter the water was cold (as was man) so he placed it near the fire in a vessel and it became warm. Then it occurred to him that cold food would become warm if placed in warm water. Some time after that someone, somewhere noticed that the water in which food had been warmed tasted even nicer than did ordinary water.

Broth has been with us ever since. It is sometimes called consommé, should accurately be described as bouillon, answers to the generic name of soup (though soup is thicker than broth) and is the result of boiling fish, flesh or vegetable etc. in water. This must be done without the addition of a designated thickening agent; rice, barley or potato can be put into a broth but it becomes soup, *de rigueur*, when it is rubbed through a sieve or liquidised.

In today's language, broth has connotations of sickness, consommé of wealth and bouillon of domestic science. Broth is good for you, everyone knows that, and broth has been good for you since they invented the printing press and published

50

guides to good nursing, and before that its qualities had been spread by word of mouth.

The rationale for the broth-is-good-for-you lobby is that food sustains and is indigestible, and broth is food made digestible by transferring its qualities from solid to liquid form. *Q.E.D.*

As one who has steadily advocated gastronomy *per se* and not as a means to some desirable state of health, I will not pursue that hare, other than to repeat that anything you eat plus a vitamin pill, and if really necessary a cup of cod liver oil and syrup of figs, is better than a rigorous health-orientated diet—and I mean better in the broad sense of enjoyable living.

I mention broth because it is likely that the aftermath of any celebration, such as the Royal Wedding, will find you with a great number of left-over ingredients which you may not instantly want to commit to the waste disposal unit.

Take the buttery fillings of meat and cheese and paste sandwiches; add to them tired salads and leftovers of salad bowls containing whatever you put into them; also any scraps of anything that you thought edible (no flags or balloons). Boil for about an hour or two with as much water as you consider right and provided you add a soup-cube and some seasoning you will have a better (or worse) Post-Royal Wedding Soup than the people next door. You also get that good feeling of being an economic housekeeper and have the base for a Bull-shot which is a splendid uplifting cocktail for the day after or the day after that.

Boil your broth until it is quite strong; let it run through a sieve; clarify it, if you want to have a little harmless fun, by boiling in it the albumen of an egg (this gathers to it all impurities so that you have a clearer—in no way better—broth) and put in a refrigerator. For a Bullshot you use this as you would tomato juice in a Bloody Mary.

If you are a genuine broth freak, you may well feel that this advice has been some way from what the French call 'sérieux', which is more earnest than is our word serious.

An olde-time broth, such as sustained our forefathers in battle while they had their leg off, was fashioned of scrag end of mutton (lamb will do), onion, potato and leek; boil for a long time with parsley stalks added late, so that the colour remains un-green and season with salt and black peppercorns. If you strain a quart of this into a pan in which you have simmered half a pound of thinly-sliced new potatoes in half-a-pint of cream, you do get a quite uncommonly delicious soup, which I dare say is very good for you. You might care to add to it a lot of freshly chopped parsley; that is good for you also.

Well, yes, I did read the Patty Hearst story: I mean, it being serialised in the *Sunday Times*, I knew it would be in the best possible taste and I would not have to hide the Weekly Review from my family as I do with the 'Opinion' column in the *Telegraph* Sunday Magazine.

So there was this incredibly rich, amazingly attractive, immaculately-bred girl with huge, well, with a substantial circumference if you ran a tape measure from a point between her shoulder-blades straight around the front and back to where you started, and she was kidnapped by the Symbionese Liberation people and blindfolded and bundled into a large cupboard in a run-down house in San Francisco, where they kept her like that for many a long week.

In this strange, cruel scenario we read with fascination of her plight and wondered: what would they give her to eat? How would the SLA provide a prisoner with a diet that ensured good health, maximum political co-operation coupled with minimum cause to have her rap on the closet door in order to inform her captors of her desire to visit the bathroom? (The English version of the episode will doubtless refer to cupboard and lavatory.)

Now I am sure I speak for the vast majority of *Sunday Times* readers when I say that the last thing in which we had an interest was her account of which members of that runcible militia did what to her, how and with what frequency. I found this unacceptably irrelevant and I am not surprised that Mr R. Murdoch has effected sweeping editorial changes at Gray's Inn Road.

To return to Ms Hearst and her sojourn in the wardrobe, the four long instalments gave a woefully inadequate analysis of the catering arrangements.

Let us personalise the situation. In the spare room of your house you hold a blindfolded high-born lady who is worth more to you alive than dead. All around, the police are searching for her—which certainly prevents you from taking the problem to a Citizens Advice Bureau. McDonald's and other take-away stores are being watched and purchasers of more than minimal orders followed and quizzed, and you do want to ensure, when you use her in a much-publicised bank robbery, that she looks her best so that people will believe that she was a willing accomplice. Bear in mind that your gang (the other members of the SLA) feels that cooking is an unworthy proletarian pastime, and the lady is blindfolded and the cupboard is dark, which rules out dishes like Peking duck and *Minestrone alla Fiorentina.*

It is a compelling problem and I think the authors of the Patty Hearst story were ill-advised to have ignored it.

It will be remembered that the Great Train Robbers were identified by the food they carelessly left behind at the farmhouse. The butcher recalled the man who had purchased a black pudding, the skin of which was found behind a dresser— or some such thing. Anyway, unusual food is out. People do not forget you if you ask for boned lamb cutlets, or half-a-pound of cheesecake and a torch.

I suppose they gave her fruit; militant pacifism goes with bananas. I doubt there was a lot of jam and cream because of the darkness. If they had any sense, which seems unlikely from what one reads, they would have given her vitamin pills and whisky which leads to health and happiness—under the circumstances.

Should you find yourself in the position of captor, or just have a guest who won't go away which puts you in the same predicament, the wisest thing might be to make a serve-all mousse and fool your shortsighted, long-staying prisoner with the variety of additions.

For the chef d'oeuvres, place one egg, one two-ounce packet

53

of Philadelphia Cream Cheese and one coffee-cupful of good oil into a liquidiser and blend till thick, which will not take long. Add two skinned fillets of smoked mackerel and one quarter-pint each of single and whipping cream and blend again. Decant this into a pretty dish and add a packet of gelatine dissolved in warm water which you mix in with a fork. Check the taste and add lemon juice, salt and pepper as you deem fit. Set in a cool place and serve in the following ways: with Cumberland sauce; another day with horseradish cream; then spread it on toast and spike with cayenne.

As the stuff gets older mix it into a garlicky mayonnaise and fill scooped-out tomatoes with the resultant cream or add sieved avocado and make it into a dip. It is the blandness of the original mixture which lends itself to such a wealth of adaptations—and Philadelphia Cream Cheese is a great product. On the label it gives the ingredients, none of which seems at first sight to be edible. Do not let this fool you; it is a tremendous stand-by—and untraceable to boot.

It was my son who introduced an Oxford contemporary with the words, 'Dad, this is Jeremy; he has had a letter published in *The Times*.' I beamed my best beam and muttered something about 'so much coming to a man so early in life . . .'

A letter to the Editor of a newspaper—one that is published and establishes the identity of the author—has long been considered an accolade of success and the higher the standing of the paper, the greater the glory.

For the writer there is something very satisfactory about spreading the word without recourse to Saatchi and Saatchi or other expensive middlemen. In fact there are people whose rise to fame and fortune and selection for participation in television programmes was occasioned solely by judiciously-timed, nicely-worded letters to the right papers. Anyone wishing to stand as a candidate for the SDP at the next election would be foolish indeed to ignore this means of bringing their claims to the attention of the parliamentary panel.

The subject-matter of the epistle is unimportant. Public

memory recalls no more than the event (like Jeremy, whose letter was published in *The Times*—a lasting and irrefutable earnest of good taste).

Ms Ann la Pla is not known to me personally—her name sounds like an anagram in an up-market crossword—but in a recent letter to the Editor of the *Daily Telegraph* she tells this good man that on a visit to her daughter at a French provincial university her baggage had been laden with tins: 'tins of steamed chocolate pudding, steamed golden syrup sponge pudding, steamed vanilla sponge pudding', and her child had said, 'Oh, Mummy, all we get here are gateaux and sorbets.'

Well, of course, it is not a very good letter, it is not even a particularly interesting letter, but if it is your desire to have a letter published in the *Daily Telegraph*, it is the ideal letter. It contains everything close to the heart of the Editor: patriotism, denigration of foreign eating habits, mistrust in British tertiary education and a touch of snobbery: who, other than an AB-class reader would call mother Mummy at the age of whatever is the current age of undergraduettes?

The more I think about it the more certain I am that this lady from Wivelsfield (yes, yes, she came from Wivelsfield) has opened up the gastro-channel to letter publication and I think it would be wrong not to grasp this nettle most vigorously. Never again will one have to explain, 'Well, yes, I did write to the *News* but I think the Editor may be sitting on the letter . . .' Food is the answer, always bearing in mind the nature of the publication.

The Editor,
The Guardian
Dear Sir,

Last week I went to call on my adopted mulatto son who is in care with a gay family in Doncaster. I brought him a parcel containing home-made muesli, apricot yogurt and sprouting bean-shoots and he said, 'Man (though I am his mother), this is really steaming stuff; out here they are deep into cheese-burgers.'

The Letters Editor,
Financial Times
Dear Sir,

My uncle, a well-known gourmand from Pontefract, recently celebrated his sixtieth birthday and I purchased for him four hundred tonnes of October futures in hog bellies. Though a Muslim, he was delighted with my gift.

The Editor,
Sporting Life
Sir,

I read with admiration your correspondent's assessment of this year's crop of three-year-olds. On a recent holiday in Belgium I noted that the *carbonnade* garnished with wild mushrooms was indeed tastier than in any year since the great Sea Bird II. Moreover, this season's *tournedos* are more handsomely marbled and more tender than ever before; this I put down to the influence of US bloodlines.

The Editor,
The Sun,
My Dear Sir,

At a sea-front café in Lowestoft my Auntie and I were served with a sherry trifle: a soft cream-coloured alcoholic base was topped by a crumbly layer which supported two luscious apricots bulging through their thin covering of custard. It was decorated with a single pink candle. I took a photograph of it but the chemist refused to release the print because of some new Act of Parliament.

Letters Editor,
Do-It-Yourself Magazine
Dear Sir,

My nine-year-old son bought a ball of Courtauld's twine, a bottle of Holt's Stop-a-Rad-leek and a $1\frac{1}{2}$-ounce tube of Polyfilla; with this he makes hamburgers which he serves with fried onions. Could the onions do any harm to consumers?

56

The Editor,
The Times
Dear Sir,
    Yesterday I ate my first cuckoo.

CHAPTER FOUR

Ideal world

In the best of all possible worlds, a menu would list the sum total of the dishes at the command of the kitchens . . . and specify the size, freshness, method of preparation, garnish and price.

Thus: *Battery chicken. Half of a 2lb 8oz beast. Slaughtered at dawn last Tuesday. Grilled with bacon. £2.75.* I accept that this takes longer to read than *Demi Poussin grillé à l'anglais* but is considerably more honest than *Plump Halves Of Idaho-Reared Baking Hen Succulently Sizzled Over Applewood, Basted With Jersey Butter And Anointed With Strips Of Lean, Pan-Fried Rashers Of Wiltshire Bacon M.P.* (this last nonsense means Market Price, or to put it another way, we shan't tell you how much it is going to cost you until we decide how rich you are).

Let me begin by pointing out that we do *not* live in the best of all possible worlds (I mean, just look around) and that the catering trade has never been in the forefront when awards for honesty were being given out; indeed how could they have been, in a business in which success is measured by the ratio between a full till and an empty pig-bin?

Unless you hit upon a winning recipe, as has the fast-growing US food chain that serves the freshest hamburgers because their only other commodity is chili con carne (which requires the most matured minced beef) there is a natural progression of usage of ageing food: the very, very fresh you can serve raw ... or display on a buffet. The very fresh you boil or grill; the fresh is pan-fried; the fairly fresh deep-fried; the less fresh stewed, the hardly-fresh-at-all curried and after that it is served to the staff. (Caterers are of course advised to take out maximum cover for customer indemnity insurance.)

I have never felt it advisable to teach people the innermost secrets of the catering trade if it is their intention to become respected restaurant customers. In those far-off days when I was a practitioner—as opposed to my present calling of peripatetic consumer—we of the starched cardboard shirt-fronts were deeply suspicious of those who knew too much and had considerable respect for the amiable moron.

The man who looked at a menu, murmured 'Filet de Sole Veronique ... let me see now ... skinned fillets of Dover Sole, poached in a white wine courtbouillon, cloaked in a velouté thickened with cream and garnished with peeled halves of white muscat grapes then flashed under the salamander' was heard in stony silence.

Far from being impressed, we felt that the man in question was odds-on to be the fish-cook having a day off from a rival establishment.

My advice is to learn a little but only so much as will convince the serving staff that you are no more than a not totally moronic customer and as the skill of eating out is to give the steady impression that if they look after you well, their attention will be richly rewarded; do work on that, too.

Little manifestations of opulence like lighting your cigarette with a rolled-up ten-pound note; promise of social desirability, like 'when the Duke phones again, please tell him I have just left', have been known to work wonders.

To return to the menu, it is sensible to learn some of the more common garnishes: *bonne femme* denotes that there are mushrooms, somewhere in the dish. Anything with the suffix *crecy* means carrots; *St Germain* denotes dried peas; *favorite*, green beans; *florentine* ... spinach; *italienne* ... tomatoes. *Provençale* spells garlic ... and so forth.

The excellent publication *Repertoire de la Cuisine* gives the composition of every dish in the classic French kitchen, though it is about as exciting reading as is the telephone directory.

There are, also, people who have endowed dishes. Dame Nellie Melba, the Australian opera singer, for instance, gave her name to the most beautiful sauce made of sieved strawberries and raspberries which is poured over fresh peaches that nestle against vanilla ice-cream . . . and, when she became enormously fat (what is now called having a weight problem) there was Toast Melba. This is *not* bread cut into thin slices and toasted, but bread cut into thinnish slices, toasted on both sides, de-rinded and then split lengthwise, after which the two newly exposed surfaces of bread are toasted.

Arnold Bennett is said to have liked smoked haddock . . . hence *omelette Arnold Bennett*. The garnish *reine* comes from La Reine Victoria, and consists of totally unamusing strips of boiled breast of chicken. And there are many restaurants that call particular dishes after good or valued or important customers . . . thus *Oeuf Poche Humperdink* or Ice Cream Goldberg.

Should it be your ambition to have a great dish called after you, it might be wise to think on the sad tale of Captain Wenberg, an American seafaring gentleman who sailed the eastern spice route and would return on leave to nineteenth-century New York. Having presented some of his booty to the chef of Del Monico's he gave his seal of approval to lobster baked in cream and spiced with his peppers and turmeric. Lobster Wenberg became a famous dish at Del Monico's . . . until the day the Captain overdid it; he became drunk and abusive, insulted the maitre d' (just as if he had been back on board, at his Captain's table) and the restaurant, as a punishment, inverted the first three letters of Wenberg's name. Lobster Newberg it has been ever since.

There *are* dishes that appear on menus in classic form on the ground that Chicken Maryland is known and recognised while deep-fried chicken garnished with corn fritters and battered bananas and pineapple and bacon is a cumbersome sentence with which to burden a menu.

However, the language of the menu is more often used to

break down or deceive the customer than to help him.

Under the latter heading, my least favourite ploy is *l'Agneau Specialité du Chef* . . . rather than, say, *Gigot d'Agneau rôti*.

If it is the latter, and you get anything but a roast of leg of lamb, you can object . . . but *'specialité du chef'* entails a tedious explanation by the waiter (which probably changes from day to day, let alone chef to chef) but allows them to get away with it—'well, burning the minced lamb is his great speciality.'

The other trick is to call dishes by such outrageous names that the very act of pronouncing them takes from the customer any right of complaint or reproach that he might previously have had.

I am thinking of *Momma Lapoccini's Delectable Yummi-yum Mammoth Slodgeburger*. Once you have said that, do you have the courage to cast reasonable doubt upon yummiyumness?

I have no ambition to lend my name to a dish—perhaps the juvenile years of Freud Fish and Freud Eggs followed by seeing my name misspelt on several million French cold water taps put paid to that—but if pressed I should go for a method, rather than a garnish with which to be associated . . .

Chicken à la Freud

Take a 2 lb chicken. Rub this with salt and fresh milled pepper. Into a saucepan large enough to take the whole chicken . . . moreover one with a well fitting lid . . . put 2lb of baby turnips, cleaned and peeled and diced into one inch dice. Also 2oz butter, salt and pepper and lemon thyme. When the turnips start sizzling, place the chicken on top of the turnips, put lid on pan, turn down the flame and let the chicken cook for an hour and a quarter in the juices and steam of the buttery turnips.

Serve the chicken, jointed, with the turnips roughly mashed with double cream. And if restaurateurs want to steal that recipe and call it Clement Freud's morning-gathered yummi-yum sun-kissed mouth-watering melt-on-your-tongue whatever, I forgive them. Moreover, they would be right.

My political colleagues would be shocked . . . but in an Ideal

World there will be an almost unlimited number of hard-working, underpaid, obedient and faithful staff.

About eating then. (I write of the Ideal World.)

Breakfast consists of a bowl of stewed Cape gooseberries and a glass of chilled juice extracted from pink Florida grapefruit. Then a pause before Grape Nuts served with soft brown sugar and gold top milk . . . in fact, there will be no other colour seal upon milk bottles. On high days and holidays an egg Benedictine—softly poached egg on grilled muffin garnished with Parma ham and decorated with and Hollandaise sauce. For weekdays warm, crisp croissants, unsalted butter and ginger marmalade.

(The Ideal World will have done away with frozen food, dried herbs, taste stimulants and preservatives quite apart from desiccated coconut and Dr Scholl sandals which had no place even in the faultiest of civilisations.)

We move smoothly to elevenses, for tea or coffee were only compromises to sobriety and have little intrinsic merit.

A ripe peach, preferably a ripe white peach, skinned, liquidised, moistened with Armagnac and topped with a half bottle of Reoderer's Crystal Brut Champagne should be served in a large Waterford glass (which you keep in a deep freeze, do you not?) and is almost bound to stave off actual hunger-pains until it is time for luncheon. Bake a few Pentland Javelin potatoes in a roasting tray covered with a layer of rock-salt; when soft cut in halves, remove most, but not all, of the soft interiors and fill the resultant cavities with spoonsful of Beluga caviare topped with a little soured cream and some hard-boiled egg yolk pressed through a sieve. You would be foolish to drink less than quite a lot of very cold Russian vodka with this.

Grouse next; grouse is available at all times of the year, all birds being plump and female. Stuff the interior with well-seasoned butter, drape a thin slice of hard pork fat over the breast and bake in a hot oven for 25 minutes before removing the fat and giving her a final 5 minutes blast of heat.

The grouse is served on a slice of brioche fried in very hot sunflower oil until crisp and golden, then spread with the heart and liver of the bird simmered in butter, minced and spiked with crushed white peppercorns.

For accompaniment to the grouse, a gravy made by dissolving the juices of the roasting pan with burgundy; a bread sauce extravagant with cream and chopped onion, soft white crumbs and a touch of ground clove . . . and golden crumbs made by toasting a cut milk loaf under a warm grill until very dry, then crushing the slices with a rolling pin.

Pommes soufflés are a pleasant accompaniment and in an ideal world they will not have to be made with the care and attention which is currently required in selecting the type of tuber, the thickness of the slice and the two temperatures of fat which cause the potato discs first to blister and then to puff.

The salad is constructed of watercress and corn—what the French call *marche* and the Germans *Rapunzel*—dressed with olive oil and rock salt and the grated rind of half a lemon. You stir until the salt is dissolved in the oil and mix with the greenery at the last moment, else the leaves will wilt. (The absence of acidity in the dressing is intended to make for greater enjoyment of the 1969 magnum of Romanee Conti.)

Complete the meal with a dish of wild strawberries and a glass of *eau de vie de framboise* from the deep freeze.

About sustenance to tide you over the afternoon void, before the arrival of the smoked swordfish canapés, the parmesan and cayenne puff pastry straws and the glass of *kir*, made by adding 1978 domaine-bottled Sancerre to a glug of *sirop de Cassis* (no, Ribena will not do). On balance I am in favour of nothing at all, so that dinner can be properly appreciated (though there is a firm in Corsicana, Texas, that bakes an amazing cake so richly packed with cherries and almonds, pineapple and angelica that one is tempted to try a slice with the tea-time Pimms.)

Colchester Number One oysters . . . with a little lemon juice.

Young green English asparagus . . . with a soft mousseline sauce.

Suckling pig, the skin scored and roasted to perfect crispness; the interior stuffed with truffled forcemeat.

New potatoes simmered in cream and chopped chives.

Ratatouilles of fresh tomatoes, sweet peppers, baby marrow, Spanish onions and aubergines baked in olive oil and white wine and fresh basil and green peppercorns and finally—

Chanterelles on toast.

The toast crisp and dry; the chanterelles, those most delectable of all edible fungi, well washed, carefully dried, before you give all those that are larger than the top joint of your little finger to the staff—and simmer the rest in a mixture of butter and bland oil until properly cooked.

Serve Poire William liqueur with the crystallised ginger; keep Grahams 1948 Vintage Port for the Farmhouse Blue Cheshire Cheese (Bath Oliver biscuits are best) and remember and be grateful that this is part of your calorie-controlled diet.

What is more, in an ideal world, Alka Seltzer will be unnecessary and silent.

Slimming causes more human misery than any other human affliction; you only have to look at the Kleinwort scale of suffering, which currently registers an all-time high of 48.4 (its previous peak, 43.7, was before the Liberal/SDP Alliance).

I speak as a man who once put on nine pounds in weight over a mere four days and if you should think less of me because there was previously even less of me, then let me remind you that prior to that I weighed about the same as I weigh now. 'I dieted. I stopped. I ate.' (As Caesar might have put it in Latin—in which it would have sounded better.)

I discovered this diet—whereby I was advised the wholehearted consumption of water biscuits over the first 24-hour period, followed by a day's slurping of unlimited amounts of dry white wine; Day Three saw you back on the biscuits, Day Four was another all-wine day and on the final day you nibbled biscuits while you weighed yourself.

Eleven pounds less, according to my scales. Unlike most people who recommend and forecast, I actually did it. I took my writing to heart—as my stomach is witness. Let me reminisce;

64

I spent Day One with flakes of Jacob's high-baked spilling from my pockets like duodenal dandruff.

Next day, I went to a race meeting and celebrated with dry white wine followed by dry white wine, regardless of the position of the horses that I supported on the track. Rumour had it that I backed six winners; fact is that I drank six bottles. The good thing about my Day Three was that one didn't feel like anything much, and in the absence of a quart of iced milk, water biscuits are not much worse than any other food. I ate water biscuits, though not with quite the abandon of the previous day-but-one due to an absence of free-running saliva. That had to wait until Day Four.

There is a lesson about Day Four: the diet must be followed by people who have no social or professional commitments of importance. Day Four for me involved two functions in ecclesiastical surroundings, at neither of which they served dry white wine. So I had the choice of drinking for my professional research, or defying the diet against the greater glory of God; I mean, who wants to be found in the vestry pantless (or, for that matter, vestless in the pantry, let alone legless in the belfry).

The good news is that the diet works sensationally over short periods of time if you can cope with a day of halitosis followed by one of inebriation. The fact is that you can probably slim if you stick to any one item of food or drink: you become sylphlike if you confine yourself to bananas—or runner beans or boiled chicken or brown bread or wine. You put on weight by a judicious mix of protein, fat and carbohydrates.

Having devised a diminishing of calorific intake, let me write a few words on a diet designed to replace lost poundage—which is altogether more amusing.

To restore five pounds in weight, why not begin with smoked salmon? (American Express will keep sending me resistible offers whereby I could have Irish linen, silver napkin rings and 2½lbs of pre-sliced fish for £94.) Best Scotch salmon costs about £1 per thinly sliced portion. With granary bread and butter and lemon juice and a large glass of dry white wine, it sets you up for the crisply roasted duck basted with salt and

65

honey. I find pints of draught Guinness a pleasant accompaniment to rich roast duck. And Marks and Spencer, in whose
underpants I am currently sitting, sell a Bramley apple pie
which is quite delicious. Brush top with melted butter, strew it
with Demerara sugar, bake it as it says on the packet for 20
minutes and serve it with very cold, slightly beaten double
cream.

If you are the sort of person who keeps a sheep, shears it and
uses the wool to knit a jacket to keep the sheep warm in the
winter, you may want to have Calvados with your apple pie.

In the best of all worlds, people would buy the product that
they liked best. They would try out the floor polishes on the
market and use the one that cleaned the floor most thoroughly
with least effort.

We do not live in the best of all possible worlds and when it
comes to consumer choice, we tend to buy what is most heavily
advertised. The big-selling floor polish now has little to do
with efficiency of performance or economy of price; much with
advertising appropriation. Spend a fortune on good TV com-
mercials and point-of-sale publicity and people are made to
feel inadequate if they are seen to buy any other floor polish.
'Still on that stuff, are you? Poor Beth. When will you learn?'

Employ a man who has convinced everyone of his brilliance
as a designer of ballistic missiles, or a breeder of dachshunds,
and have him look into camera, saying, 'Madge has found that
Slippyglo gives a long-lasting effortless shine, which enables
her to get to the tennis club before the nightwatchman leaves,'
and the stuff is on the way to becoming a brand leader. Life
is too full of choice for us to be able to afford, socially or
morally, to ignore the honest message—especially if it comes
at us eight times a day via a face we have learnt to love, trust,
respect or laugh with.

Lately, there has come upon the scene a new departure in
consumer advice, designed, I have no doubt, to confuse people
even more. This one is financed by the media and not the manufacturer. It is called The Test. The *Observer* colour magazine

started it with three people who tried six varieties of baked beans, of instant coffee and of tomato soup, and assessed each brand in their unique way—which is jolly useful if you know the taste of the critic and totally useless otherwise. The 'experts' taste 'blind', that is, they do not know when they slurp their instant coffee whether it is the one that rolls off David Niven's fingers, or that which soothes the long distance truck driver when he returns home after losing his EEC HGV licence after a fight at the Belgian border. .

The arbiters of taste are currently a professional chef, a lady cook and a voice on the BBC. My question is, will Shopper's Paradise oxtail soup taste any better because one or other of these dumdums (seldom both, never all) has said that it had 'a most acceptable colour, nice smell' while a similar product from International Stores was 'too thick, unimaginatively seasoned'. (Do they not realise that soups are not to be drunk straight from the tin—and thickness, flavour and colour are a challenge to water, salt and Worcester sauce?)

The *Express* magazine, the one that comes out on a Sunday to make up for John Junor, now has a wine panel consisting of two masters of wine, a man who once played a lush in a TV sitcom and someone else; as yet no black and no woman. I wish them well (I wish everyone well because the sun is shining and in six weeks I go on holiday), but wonder whether it is worth it. You have this dinner, serve them ferret's piss and as their honest faces screw up in vineous disgust, you say, 'This is the one which Panelist Number Two thought fragrantly sound with just a slight, though acceptable, overtone of fruit.'

The whole concept is a terrible insult to readers, quite apart from the fact that editors have given insufficient thought to the identity of the panelists, let alone the range of products to be tested. Above all, they have not explained—and this is the most important part if the aim is to help, rather than confuse—how they can buy economical products and improve on them.

The publishers are torn between readability, entertainment, controversy and consumer protection, and have fallen ignominiously between four stools.

A good panel would consist of the Ayatollah Khomeini, Trevor McDonald, Dr Cruise Haut Brion and an Environmental Health Officer (female). That provides a bit of balance, a snatch of knowledge, a touch of class, a nice social/ethnic spread and a virtual certainty that no two are going to feel similarly about the same product. As the poet said, one man's nectar is another man's hogwash. What would be helpful, to revert to the *Observer*, whose panel is at least replete with people who earn their living practising or pontificating on the subject of food, is not to make readers race around fifteen neighbourhood shopping arcades to find the tins or jars that they criticised but to take a dish and show how imagination and expertise can make it more delicious.

Let us try with a banana milk shake.

Put into a blender half a banana, one level dessertspoon of sugar, four ice cubes and one third of a pint of milk. Put on a high speed whizz and sieve into a tall glass just before all the ice cubes have been pulverised.

The Chancellor of the Duchy of Lancaster (*standing in for Trevor McDonald who is this week's Religious Correspondent*): 'I use a scoop of vanilla ice cream and a spoonful of Crème de Noyeau. No ice cubes—and rub the rim of the glass with lemon juice, then twist the rim in caster sugar.'

The Ayatollah Khomeini: 'Why they no use oil?' After he was assured that a milk sheikh was no political threat to anyone, he suggested that the confection would become more nourishing with the addition of wheatgerm.

Henry Cooper (*Dr Haut Brion is in Ireland*) was not available for comment.

The Environmental Health Officer is on strike.

Quite a long time ago, when calypso singers were singing 'Back to Back' and John Freeman had a television programme called 'Face to Face'—before Stephen Sondheim wrote 'Side by Side'—I had the idea of doing a programme called 'Stomach to Stomach'. It was to be a half hour (or 26½ minutes if bought by ITV) devoted to establishing the gastronomic persona of a guest, rather like 'Desert Island Disc' without the music.

I got as far as doing a pilot of the show with Marty Feldman, which did not work because I tried to be funny and Marty Feldman tried to cook. Nevertheless, it is a good idea and when I see the new issue of television personalities like Barbara Woodhouse and Lord Spencer I wonder what sort of subjects they would be for 'Stomach to Stomach':

'Tell me how you feel about waiters?'

'I tell them to SIT.'

'Do you tip them well, if they have been good?'

'I give them a bone.'

It was Brillat-Savarin who said that he could tell what a man was if you told him what the man ate; a statement that becomes sillier the more you think about it. You can tell how rich he is or how greedy or how weak; that is about it.

But in 'S to S' I was going to quiz Laurence Olivier about his liking for carrots and get Barbara Cartland to talk about bread-and-butter pudding and how many oysters she needs to write a romantic novel. What does Tom Stoppard eat when he gets home after his first nights? Is there a connection between Angela Rippon's diet and that of Enoch Powell, or are their similarities confined to politics?

In the House of Commons, where everything that goes on has party political overtones, the Labour tables eat puddings while the cheese trolley trundles unequivocally among the Tories and Liberals. The waiters knew who was going to defect to the Social Democrats long before the announcements were made; they started ordering dressed crab from the *à la carte* menu and stopped drinking house wine and asked about savouries.

Upon whether this was cause or effect I am not prepared to take a view. Could the anchovy on toast have been what gave them the final push to moderation or was it their new-found ethos that caused them to eschew ride pudding with apricot jam? (Our menus are all English now.)

To return to the food programme, the main trouble is that while people have definite views about music, a well-informed bully can make almost anyone change their mind about food.

69

'I would like to start my best summer luncheon with cold *ratatouille*,' says the victim.

'Well now,' says the interviewer, 'the mixture of tomatoes, over-ripe sweet peppers and aubergines macerated in garlic and oil makes it virtually impossible to retain any taste for later dishes and incidentally ruins the palate for the appreciation of wine. What sort of wine were you going to drink with *ratatouille*?'

'Claret.'

'A noble growth of fermented grape, one of the great artistic achievements of the vintner's expertise gulped with an oily garlicky pulp? What will you have as your next course?'

The Robin Day-like presenter will not find it easy to persuade people to appear.

For the programme to work you would have to have a format of six minutes of chat about food, eight minutes of cooking followed by eight minutes of eating—with a final session such as they had in *Perry Mason* when all the characters sat around and the plot was explained to those who were not very bright or had confused the murderer with the man on the police switchboard.

The blow to producers is that many of the more interesting of today's personalities feel that food and drink are unimportant. The awful Benn started it. He chain-smokes pipes, confines his intake to sandwiches and likes tea; teetotal with it. You could finish him off in the commercial break.

Melvyn Bragg would appear to be a splendid subject: handsome, witty, debonair but smokes cigars at breakfast. Who would want to know about the food-fads of one who smells of an ashtray before the sun has risen high enough to have a good look around?

The main problem is the Briton's pervasive courtesy which causes him to declare that everything is really very nice and prevents him from declaring how much he hates liver because his hostess gave it to him at dinner last week (gave him the liver, I mean).

Re-reading Wodehouse the other day I was struck by his reference to the members of Drones as the Crumpets, Eggs,

70

Chelsea Buns etc. This, of course, is waiter's talk. 'Thick-toast man has just come in with double-gin-and-tonic-without-lemon lady,' they say to each other, often going as far as bringing you the food with the helpful question of 'Now which one of you is the stuffed avocado?' 'Stomach to Stomach' is going to make that all better. Viewers will know who eats what and why and what made him decide to do so. Instead of having people referred to as Schoenberg or Country and Western or Reggae types, they will become Heinz Tomato Soup, or Peanut Butter and Jelly folk.

In time, gossip writers will concentrate not on the identity of the person with whom you live but the quality of what you eat and when and with what sauce served on what sort of china to be consumed with which kind of cutlery. It will be no more interesting but it may just let a whole new bunch of people into the gossip business. It will also mean that we shall have men around us who are fat and on the whole these not only need all the help we can give them, but are far more televisual than the Kurt Waldheims of the world. Mr Waldheim drinks lemon tea.

I travelled on a holiday charter flight and the as-promised-on-the-brochure-in-flight-snack was packed in a red cardboard box which crouched in a compartment set into the back of the seat in front. It contained half a dozen slices of good meat and ox tongue; some very appetising potato salad, also bread and butter and a smashing slice of English ethnic pastry. Wine was served by a surly stewardess who had joined the airline because she had seen *Airport* and wanted to marry a pilot.

Then I travelled on British Rail, under the surveillance of a guard who was a frustrated announcer; a latter-day, Macdonald Hobley of 'Where Are They Now' fame who told us very much more than we really wanted to know.

'This is the Euston train,' he said when it was too late to do anything about it. Then 'First-class accommodation is at the rear,' 'We are about to approach Runcorn,' and finally 'The buffet is now open.'

I went to the buffet remembering the red box (actually boxes because I nicked the one intended for whoever would have sat next to me had he caught the plane) but there was no meat; no salads either. No pastry. Just lots of sandwiches, conceived in plastic wrap; also biscuits in packets and apples in cling-foil.

The nice young man behind the counter promised that if I waited until the queue got shorter he would make me a toasted cheese sandwich and I took him up on his offer and I was sorry. It was not so much toasted as saunaed. Dry heat had melted soft white bread into unrelenting hard cheese; the edges were brown and the whole confection was sealed in a paper napkin, most of which I ate.

I do not know the financial logistics of catering in transit—but a buffet car presumably has to pay its way at so much a travelling hour plus depreciation, plus staff wages, plus food costs . . . upon which basis BR catering operations cannot be very profitable.

But need the food really be so unimaginative? Has the whole concept got to be such a disaster? On the whole, rail stewards are nicer than air stewardesses, perhaps because they did not go into the job for the glamour. (Come to think of it, I have never heard of a BR steward even walking out with the engine driver.)

Let me tell whoever is up there doing what he does, that the average traveller would prefer almost anything to the currently available ready-made sandwiches. How about Scotch baps which are large, soft, flattish bread-rolls and can be freshened up in the oven if they get stale? Ten-gram tubs of butter, packets of sliced beef or ham or chicken or tongue; tubes of mustard; cartons of pickle and chutney, all with plastic knives so that passengers can do their own assembly jobs.

Why cannot BR do a deal with our apple growers and our farmhouse cheese manufacturers? A Cox's Orange Pippin with a slice of strong Cheddar would be enough for me to forgive ICI for the inevitable wrapping. Meat pies seem to be the buffet car's faithful standby—or could it be the same meat pie? As Maurice Chevalier said, 'I remember it well.' Oxo, Bovril and Marmite are all more acceptable drinks than the cup of soup which is resurrected from enriched, starch-laden, mono-sodium glutamate-based powder. Boxes of Mr Kipling's cakes, tarts and fruit slices are better by far than the BR cakes—and why are there no macaroons? If they can sauna bread, why cannot they serve crumpets? Or pizzas?

In a land-bound restaurant you never have much idea of when, even whether, your customers are going to turn up: will it be before the theatre, at 9 p.m. or just as you are about to lock the doors? On a train you know the departure time to the minute, and even if the train does not actually depart at that minute, the customers are there. Could they not bring a few freshly-baked doughnuts to Lime Street's Platform 9 for the 12.46? If we, as a nation, feel that it is all right to stop an express train at a wayside station so that VIPs may get off, why not halt the train so that it can take on board a batch of newly-baked pasties or a crate of hot and succulent spare ribs? Have they investigated on-rail re-fuelling? Have they spent enough time thinking about the whole concept of trav-ellers' fare or do they just sub-contract the advertising?

If you could put the delicatessen counter of our local Key-market on wheels, the trade would be constant and enthusiastic. You only have to watch the envy on the faces of people as wise passengers unwrap their tuckabags to know that the market is there. It is the product that is missing.

CHAPTER FIVE

Monomanias

If I were writing an article about lemons for a colour supplement, in the centre of the page would be a great bowl of lemons and to one side a few slices of lemon, some lemon peel, curlicues of lemon zest, a tumblerful of lemon juice, a pot of lemon marmalade, and as the remit is simply to fill a page or two, there would not have to be too many words to detract from the pictures: 'pix' as they are known in the trade.

Writing about lemons in black and white is different, also more difficult and certainly more time-consuming.

The lemon has never had it easy when it came to presenting a public image: it is a food and a drink; sweet and acid; cherished by some for its peel, by others for its juice. It gives zing to what is bland, freshens what is stale, cleans wooden surfaces, removes ink stains from linen, can be used as a post-shampoo rinse, replaces vinegar in salad dressings, thickens mayonnaise, curdles cream, and does the most awful things to marble. *Never* leave a slice of lemon on a marble surface.

As if those qualities were not reason enough for a schizoid citrus, lemons start out green, become yellow and finish up a dull orange colour; they can be soft and juicy, or hard and dry, and occasionally hard and juicy, sometimes soft and almost dry. The retail price gravitates from 20p to 3p, unless you go to Portugal where they cannot give them away.

Having said all that, let me add that life without lemons is hardly any life at all.

On which subject, I witnessed the death of a man for comparing a nation to a lemon. It was in 1970, in Mexico City where the home team had beaten El Salvador in a first-round match of the World Cup. There was dancing in the streets and much sounding of klaxons and embracing of strangers to celebrate the 1–0 victory, and in this café in which I sat a man was shot, dead.

I read in the following day's paper that he had turned to his jubilant companions and said: 'El Salvador is a lemon' (which probably sounded slightly better in Spanish). The judge, after hearing the evidence, found that there was sufficient justifiable provocation for the man with the gun to have acted as he did, and sentenced him to some insignificant term in an open prison; adding that the deceased had been largely responsible for his own demise.

Lemon is clearly a word of which to be careful in Central America; in the rest of the world, a man without a lemon is a lesser man.

Citron pressé is one of the great soft drinks of the world. The juice of two ripe lemons passed through a sieve, mixed with two rounded tablespoons of sugar, stirred until the sugar dissolves, topped with half a pint of cold water and six ice cubes, will nicely fill two ten-ounce tumblers. Rub the rim of the tumblers with lemon rind and dunk in caster sugar to give a frosted top.

Lemon chicken is excellent—both hot and cold. You grate the rinds of three lemons into four ounces of butter and smear it around a plump battery chicken. Cut the lemons into slices and place around the chick which you then wrap in foil, and cook in a slow oven for an hour and a half. Remove foil, baste with buttery lemon and give another ten minutes in the oven.

The best sauce to go with this is simply a good rich white sauce into which you pour the lemony butter in which the chicken has been cooked. Sprigs of parsley introduce a pretty new colour into this dish.

As lemons do not improve much in the warm weather, it is a good idea to keep them in the refrigerator; and if you should have a large freezer, an excellent idea is to buy when they are cheap and keep a few dozen deep frozen. They can be revived over the months and, if they should be needed quickly, a frozen lemon can be brought to life simply by boiling it in water. Nothing deteriorates and if you should want lemon to provide a slice thereof for a gin and tonic, you need not even thaw it; just use a saw to carve yourself a cooling slice.

As some very nice people sent me a basket of avocados the other day, it is only fair to say that avocados and lemon juice are an excellent starter, and if you have not tried avocados with the centre cavity filled with sugar and the sugar flooded with lemon juice, you might have missed what I consider to be one of the very best ways of eating avocados.

I knew a man who maintained that no one of discretion ate ice-cream just as it came from the packet. Commercial ice-cream was a base, he maintained (this was before the days of speciality ice-creams) and I took it to heart and had much success with Walls Family Bricks (vanilla) into which I mixed a concoction made of grated rind of one lemon and one tablespoon of caster sugar dissolved in one tablespoon of lemon juice. I made the additive in advance, mixed with a fork at the last moment, and the hardest part of the exercise was disposing of the tell-tale cardboard wrapper.

I would now venture to suggest that discriminating people ignore the instructions printed upon the labels of Colman's Mustard, double superfine (warranted pure). Let me remind you of the words and apologise to Messrs Reckitt and Colman Ltd if they are copyright:

'Mix gradually with COLD WATER' (their capitals) 'to the consistency of very thick cream, stirring well and breaking up all lumps; then let it stand for ten minutes to develop full flavour.'

I quite like the word 'mix'; certainly would not argue with it. 'Gradually' is absurd. The ratio of mustard powder to liquid is about two to one. If you mix 'gradually' you begin by making something the consistency of soft cement before gradually diluting it to the desired creaminess. Take two level spoonfuls of mustard, one of liquid and mix, would make sense.

'COLD WATER', even 'cold water', defeats me. I have just made three lots of mustard, one with cold, one with tepid, the third with boiling water. There is not a jot of difference between them, though the boiling water mustard smelled more potent than the other two for the first two minutes. After ten minutes they were identical.

I don't go a lot for 'the consistency of thick cream' but accept 'stirring well and breaking up all lumps'; I mean that is what inevitably happens when you stir liquid into a powder, especially if you do it well. It's the final enjoinder, the bit after the semi-colon, to which I really take exception. 'Let it stand ten minutes to develop full flavour.' The intimation is quite clearly that for the first ten minutes the flavour is less than full and that after the magic six hundred seconds, it begins to empty.

I wonder how they came to that conclusion: could it be that a dozen Colmen assembled in their Norwich boardroom, each with a pot of mustard made by gradually mixing, etc.; that they tasted the very thick cream-like substance at one-minute intervals and after the tenth slurp they shouted, '*This is it*'? Or was it that at the eleventh tasting they shook their heads in sorrow and muttered, '*It's gone*'?

I just hope that they were not trying to sod up people's dinners, because the one thing you DO NOT (my capitals) want to do ten minutes before eating meat is make mustard. (If the instructions are for people's servants, this is a different matter and they should have said so.)

Let me now state that I am a fan of Messrs Colman's Mustard powder and to some extent of their ready-made mustard, though I fail to see how they can decently sell it in view of their ten-minute rule. My advice to you is to buy it in large quantities—I have a 4lb square tin—because dry mustard keeps for a very long time, so long as you close the tin firmly.

And don't use water, either hot or cold, unless you have tried and rejected other liquids. Milk is good. The blandness of the milk takes some of the worst sharpness from the mustard and the mixture will retain its creaminess long after the mustard-made-with-water has formed a dark yellow skin and dried up. If you like the sharpness of mustard, make it with milk and add a dash of Tabasco, some cayenne pepper or freshly grated horseradish.

The reason why we spend so many millions of pounds annually importing French and German mustards (and they spend so few millions importing ours) is because people read the legend on Colman's label and try it and look elsewhere.

This is foolish. Mustard is mustard is mustard. Buying Colman's is like buying pure alcohol—and complaining that it is too strong and too nasty. With a tin of Colman's you have the whole mustard world at your feet—and not just for ten minutes, either. Make your own mixture, keep it in an air-tight pot and if you get hooked on your own home-made mustard you can buy glycerine or emulsifiers to keep it as desirable as commercial mustards sold in jars.

To begin with, try: six dessertspoons of mustard powder, half that quantity of plain yoghourt and a teaspoonful of honey or golden syrup. For variety, make anchovy mustard with essence, or sieved anchovy fillets—a marvellous accompaniment to grilled mackerel or herrings. If you like mustard with lamb, make a mint mustard or even a red-currant jelly mustard. (Melt the jelly . . . else you will have to stir VERY VERY well to break up all lumps.)

P.S. Next time you drive into the country and feel warm and proud at the sight of those billowing fields of yellow about which A. E. Coppard wrote so evocatively, the odds are that they aren't mustard. It's rape seed which makes the world smell like linoleum and without which you might not be able to have as much margarine as the producers and their advertising agents would like.

In the first year of the war—well the first year of my war, other, older people had been fighting for some time—I spent a weekend at a house on the outskirts of Oxford and the host said, 'You know about food; I've got a chicken.' It transpired that his cook had been in the Army since 1939.

Now 'I've got a chicken' would hardly raise a cheer in these battery-orientated times in which we live, but in 1943 the phrase commanded respect, admiration, envy and considerable loyalty.

'I also,' said the host, knowing when he was on to a good thing, 'have eggs and some top of the milk.' That night we had a feast which I have not forgotten; though the chicken was an old, tough rooster I simmered him in water and cider and salt and an onion spiked with cloves for all of three hours.

I then took the meat from the bones, put it into a warm oven and reduced the skin and bones and chicken stock and strained it on to the egg-yolks beaten into the cream. (Had there been lemon, I would have added lemon but there were none in those hard years of my youth.) It was a very memorable feast and even today when people say 'Chicken?' I think of that evening nostalgically before I say, 'No, thank you.'

It is not only that chicken has ceased to be the good animal it was; even tradesmen are ashamed of it. If a fishmonger sold legs of lamb or joints of beef, the butchery trade would be up in arms, but at Mac Fisheries the chicken lies on the slab next to the haddock and no one says a word. A butcher exhibits whole lambs and the occasional pig's head with marbles stuck in the sockets where the eyes had been; it is done for realism. But a chicken is presented upside down, head removed, neck stuffed up its back passage, innards hidden away in a plastic bag and legs rubber-banded against the breast. That way no one will be moved to say, 'How cruel to eat a chicken' (though anyone who has ever had anything to do with chickens will tell you that, along with ferrets and earwigs, they are among the unloveliest creatures of the animal kingdom).

The fact is that the chicken is presented as inexpensive, antiseptic, dead meat and over the years people have given it the attention such an inanimate object appeared to deserve.

Over 70 per cent of today's domestic chicken sales go to households where the form is to roast it, carve it —and put it back into the oven. Roast chicken attracts Bisto—as a salvation rather than an accompaniment.

As for boiled chicken, it is as good—and not a jot better—than the stock in which you boiled the brute, unless you are going to get a real bird that led something of a social life in a farmyard rather than one of its cousins who never knew the time of day.

When my eldest daughter said, 'Come and have lunch,' and took me to a Chinese restaurant and ordered—and I got chicken—I said, 'How nice; chicken,' and had it not been for the pitch of my voice I could easily have been mistaken for Her Majesty the Queen Mother. But it was nice, and not because it had pursued a rich uplifting life but because the Chinese chef had said, 'This meat tastes of nothing at all; it is a challenge.' The dish was called Ginger Chicken and the fierce joy of the root had pervaded the meat while the slow and careful process of cooking it had made it swell rather than shrink. Can you imagine swollen slivers of plump white meat redolent of the spices of the East? The Chelsea Rendezvous Ginger Chicken had it all.

Dewhursts, the butchers who fly the proud banner of the Vestry family, sell fowl at 44p a pound, frozen, which is a totally temporary condition if you have central heating or a refrigerator that does not work very well. Bear in mind that nothing you do to a chicken can make it much worse than it usually is, so you have little to lose. There is much to be gained from experiment.

If you like tarragon chicken, a roasted bird swathed in buttery tarragon leaves, given an hour and a quarter on gas mark 6, still tastes of not very much. But leave the beast in oil and tarragon and crushed peppercorns for a day or two and then joint it and remove the skin (which is much easier after a sojourn in marinade); add some sherry or vermouth and tabasco and leave it for another day before you cook it in its own juices in a cool oven for quite a long time. People will begin to talk about you as one of those gourmet fellows.

Serve it with rice and boil up the chicken juices with equal parts of dry white wine and double cream and forty years from now people will write about you in culinary appreciations that begin: 'In the last months before the outbreak of Ronald Reagan—on me, he had broken out over the people of California some years previously— . . .'

Dr Rhodes Boyson who used to be a headmaster but is one no longer, steadily refers to children as 'chillun'; whereas he once taught chillun, he now administers the ever-increasing number of disadvantaged chillun in the public sector of education—though he is a great supporter of the Assisted Places scheme whereby chillun in maintained schools will be sent into the private sector at public cost. 'Good for the chillun,' his verdict.

Bernard Matthews, who has actually done significantly more for turkeys than Boyson ever did for Youth, talks of the vehicle of his fame and fortune as 'durkeys'. 'Real Norfolk durkeys', also durkey rolls, smoked durkey, whole ranges of durkey products; and he looks at us from the TV screen like a man who knows what he is on about *and* refers to himself in the third person, a sure sign of having arrived. (Why is it that 'talking turkey' means straight talk while in America 'a turkey' is a term of extreme political and social denigration?)

I have had recent occasion to become involved with turkeys. A constituent purchased a few acres of farmland on the outskirts of a village and applied for planning permission for two houses.

'Not on your Nellie,' said the District Council.

'It is for a turkey farm,' said my constituent, 'and my foreman and I have to live on the premises in case anything ugly happens to the birds.'

The District Council gave him conditional permission to build, the building consent being subject to the presence of turkeys. My constituent appealed, because no building society would lend him money to erect dwelling houses which could be demolished by the enforcement officer in the absence of turkeys, and the Department of the Environment allowed the appeal—which sets a very interesting precedent: as a responsible Member of Parliament I will now have to advise all my clients who complain to me about refusal of planning permission to consider the turkey alternative.

To return to gastronomy, Brillat-Savarin wrote, 'In my Secret Memoirs I find sundry notes recording that on many occasions the turkey's restorative juice has illumined diplomatic faces of the highest eminence.' Of course the main problem about today's birds is that they don't have a lot of juice with which to restore anyone. In fact there is no good reason why a twenty-week turkey, which by man's genius has been translated from three-and-a-half ounce egg to thirty-pound monster of the BUT666 variety (sounds more like a cherished number-plate than a Christmas dinner), should be juicy, let alone taste of anything more exciting than fishmeal and droppings. And yet this need not be so.

Mr Bernard Matthews's smoked durkeys are marvellously moist and succulent, and if Brillat-Savarin had extended illumination to embrace politics, just the sort of thing one should send to cheer up Sir Keith.

In the heyday of *haute cuisine*, the quality of a turkey depended on the length of time it had been hung with its innards left *in situ*. Today the liver, heart, lights *et al* are whipped out within a few minutes of killing and plucking, and although there is a gastro-gaggle around Papworth Everard which buys turkey giblets, stuffs them into defrosted birds and hangs them for a few days in an outhouse, this seems to me an unnecessary extravagance.

If it is turkey-based juice that you are after, especially juice combined with succulent meat, then roasting today's bird is a mistake. Let me advise you to boil the brute very slowly in the most handsomely constructed broth. You might like to stuff it before boiling, in which case equal parts of minced veal, minced lean pork and white breadcrumbs should be bound with beaten egg (two eggs per $1\frac{1}{2}$lb of stuffing) and flavoured with fresh herbs and lemon juice and salt and quite a lot of freshly ground pepper. Truss the turkey well, or wrap him in a cloth of butter muslin tightly knotted to draw the legs into the body and prevent the stuffing from dropping into the liquor.

Put the turkey into the smallest saucepan that will accommodate it—that is ever the way to producing high-quality broth. Add cold water to cover the whole bird and add one chopped onion, a few sticks of celery, a leek, cut up, one medium-sized carrot, four cloves, twelve peppercorns and a small bunch of parsley.

Bring to the boil, cover the pan and simmer for two hours for a 10-pound bird; two and a half hours if it weighed 14 pounds. For the sauce, take one pint of the turkey stock, add a glass of dry white wine or Bulmer's Number 7 extra dry still cider and reduce to two-thirds of the volume by boiling. Thicken with double cream if you are rich, or flour and butter if things are hard. Should you have some turkey and sauce left over, add gelatine to the lukewarm cream sauce and when it is dissolved, but the sauce still warm, pour it over turkey portions and set these in a cool place.

My eldest daughter telephoned me the other day and said, 'There is nothing about Steak Tartare in your cookery book.'

'Not in *Freud on Food* in paperback priced £1.50, available at good booksellers with a picture of the author on the cover?' I asked.

'No,' she said.

So I looked at some other cookery books and noticed that they had nothing about it either . . . with the exception of Larousse, who really should not have tried. Under Beefsteak Tartare he says, 'Proceed as described in the recipe for Beefsteak *à l'americaine* but omit the raw yolk.' And under that receipt the author says:

'Trim three-quarters of a pound (400 grams) of fillet of beef. Cut off fat, chop the meat finely and shape into four round flat little cakes. Put them on a serving dish. Make a little nest in the centre of each steak and slip a raw yolk into it. Serve separately chopped onion, parsley and capers pickled in vinegar. The dish is often prescribed in a building-up diet.'

I would describe this as an object lesson in how not to write a recipe. It is not just that three-quarters of a pound is *not* 400 grams; that trimming a fillet means cutting off the fat, so what the hell else do you trim for; that if you suggest a quantity for the meat, how about one for the onion, capers and parsley; if you want to suggest a 100-gram steak why not say so instead of shaping four out of 400? How about salt and pepper? And why 'put them on a serving dish'? Surely, with so little information, the reader would have guessed that Larousse did not intend you to balance them on the bathroom towel rail. Also, if the meat is going to be shaped into 'little' steaks, is it really important to state that you should make a 'little' nest in the centre of each?

I have no personal grudge against Larousse. I just hate the pretentious, boring, pontificating, pedantic, endlessly cross-referencing, shoddily-indexed publication.

To return to Steak Tartare, this is more a way of life than a strict recipe. Man's greatest compliment to man, in the days before they changed the law, was to eat him. You never ate people you did not like or respect and you ate your friends in the most atavistic form—ideally well-hung, drained of blood, with sinews drawn but without additives like ginger, and no accompaniments such as pancakes or Yorkshire pudding. Man was served neat.

Well, Steak Tartare is man's compliment to cattle and you eat your raw beef in any way that you care, remembering that unlike cannibalism the act of consuming beef is not done for any ulterior motive, like admiration for the soul of the beast. And you don't use fillet unless you have more brass than brains, as they say in Rochdale. (I know this because I share an office with Cyril Smith when one or other of us is there.) Rump is best, rump has more taste, disproving the theory that the greater the proximity to the head, the better is the eating. (This does apply to lamb, where the taste of shoulder *is* superior to that of leg. But as you are going to grate the meat, topside or skirting, which is sometimes called flank, produces excellent results.)

If you order Steak Tartare in the best restaurants, the head waiter—or whoever—will come and do the whole thing under

84

your critical gaze. He takes about 300 grams of ground beef per person, depresses the centre with a soup spoon and puts in one egg yolk. (The Larousse proportion of a yolk to 100 grams is cloying and undesirable.) He then drips oil on to the yolk while mixing vigorously with a fork. This entitles him to a tip at the end of the evening, but anyone with a grain of common sense would realise that a spoonful of mayonnaise is a better, more practical, less cumbersome idea.

Blend a rounded tablespoon of mayonnaise into the 10 ounces of meat and add salt, freshly-ground pepper, Tabasco, Worcester sauce; also very finely chopped onions, capers and fresh parsley (if all you have is dried parsley, do not bother your meat with it) and then add lemon juice, mix well and taste the mixture frequently so that you get the flavour that you care for. Stand the Steak Tartare in a cool place for a few minutes and make enough breakfast toast, because you eat Steak Tartare as you eat pâté.

Wise men do not drink rich wines with a dish like this, because raw onion, Worcester sauce and Tabasco make it hard to tell a great wine from a good one. I recently drank a Monlot-Capet 1976 St Emilion—much more suitable for seasoned beef than is a Lafite 1970. On the subject of Worcester sauce, try putting a drop on a copper coin, such as a 2p piece, and see what it does to that after leacing it for a minute. Then imagine what effect the stuff will have on your stomach.

Whoever was responsible for design of the human race certainly did a fine job; and you cannot blame our forefathers for their desire to eat each other.

If I were asked which eight sauces I would take with me to a desert island, I should bear in mind that the content is of secondary importance to the legend—and begin by selecting Brand's A1.

About half way through the narrative on the label are the immortal words: ' "Brand," said the King, "this Sauce is A1" and so it has remained to this day.'

The blurb seems to me to pose more questions than it

answers: was the King—it was George III—sane at the time? Was Brand eating in the dining room, or could His Majesty have been in the kitchen? What was *under* the sauce and why is it not mentioned . . . or did the King eat sauce neat?

I should also take with me Hellmann's mayonnaise. 'Making real mayonnaise,' it says on the label, 'is an art which has taken Hellmann's a very long time to perfect. We take eggs, the purest vegetable oil and the finest flavourings. We blend them together with patience and skill into creamy light Hellmann's mayonnaise.'

Now, I have not been to Hellmann's works but I would be surprised to find a lot of contemplative chefs opening small parcels of fine ingredients and adding them judiciously to the purest of oils that have been patiently blended with egg.

As a gourmet, I recognise some of the fine flavourings—like salt, pepper and vinegar. I also recognise the 'pure' oil and would ask the manufacturers to bear in mind the appeal of impure oil, like olive or walnut, with all the attendant taste that goes with impurity. Real mayonnaise is another misnomer, if you believe every cookery book written before liquidisers were invented, for it was they who added albumen to yolk in the line-up of ingredients. *Real real* mayonnaise uses only the yolk. Before Hellmann's friends, family and supporters get angry, let me confirm that theirs is probably the most acceptable of bottled mayonnaises. Let me also state that anyone with a blender can do as well, without patience or skill, at about half the cost.

The invention of mayonnaise is one of the wonders of culinary art: its discovery entailed the separation of yolk from white (who would want to do that?); and then the dripping of oil on to the yolks while the mass was vigorously worked with a whisk-like apparatus. Even then the mixture, though thick, needs acid to make it palatable and sauce-like, salt for flavouring and extra thickness. It makes one wonder at discoveries still to come.

Tales of a defective cork stuck into the oil bottle reducing the flow to a trickle, an old egg in which the albumen stuck to and remained in the shell and a chef with St Vitus' Dance still

86

set you wondering what he was doing pouring the oil on the egg in the first place.

While Hellmann's are patiently, skilfully blending away at their light creamy product, try boiling up two tablespoonfuls of vinegar with four of water and one teaspoon of sugar. When this has been reduced to two tablespoons in toto, put one whole egg and one egg yolk into a blender, whizz it at the lowest speed, trickle on the boiled vinegar and add half a pint of bland salad oil in a thin jet; the operation should take about ten seconds.

Remove the sauce from the blender, add a little lemon juice and some salt and mix it and taste it and add mustard if you like mustard; similarly, cayenne pepper.

What you have not got, which Hellmann's have, is a jar with a label or an ingredient that will make the mayonnaise keep in good shape for a week or more. I have never wanted mayonnaise to keep for a week or more; I have found last week's mayonnaise less appetising than this week's, but if you want to give it an application of what will make it stay thick and off-white and never disclose to anyone that it was once oil and egg, write to me in a plain envelope and I will disclose the secret of preservatives.

On the subject of adding things to mayonnaise, an adequate amount of gelatin dissolved in accordance with instructions on the packet is a good way of increasing what caterers call the 'visual desirability' or 'eye appeal' of a dish. I mean a tin of tunnyfish, one of sweet peppers chopped, and one of small garden peas to which you add liquid mayonnaise, makes a sloppy though colourful salad. Add gelatin, decant the slop into six small bowls and after a sojourn in the refrigerator tip each on to a lettuce leaf and you have a good-looking starter.

I learn from *The Little Green Book*, which someone left in my bathroom, that in the course of a lifetime each of us Britons consumes 56 sheep, 36 pigs, 8 cattle and 550 poultry.

If you bear in mind that the average British sheep, in the course of its lifetime, consumes 58 football pitches, the average pig eats $13\frac{1}{2}$ sheep, the average cow takes on board three-quarters of a metric tonne of fish and the average chicken does not interest me at all, you will understand why I am toying with a vegetarian way of life.

There are drawbacks: I don't have sandals. Also I like meat, especially meat which comes from football-pitch-eating animals —though I make an exception of Home Park, Plymouth, where the cattle can go straight ahead and eat the pitch, the players *and* the manager. However, I would like to do something significantly ecological in the coming year—though whatever it is must not annoy the members of the March and Chatteris branches of the National Farmers Union who annually invite me to dinner.

After considerable deliberations, I have decided to make this the year of celery. I shall become celeriac. Celery is quick, clean, health-giving, organic, orgasmic, fibrous and rich in phosphates as well as Vitamins A, B, D_4 and M. Come December the movement is going to be jolly proud of me— which will be reciprocated, because of all that fibre. The trouble about going celeriac for a twelvemonth is the possibility of becoming bored with the stuff and this is where being a gourmet is such a tremendous help.

Celery Soup for 11
Take one large marrow-bone, 2lb oxtail, 2lb rough-chopped onion and roast on a greased tray for half an hour in a hot oven. Decant contents of tray into 8 pints water, simmer for 1 hour, reduce to half its volume by fast boiling and season to taste. Strain the broth on to 8 ounces finely chopped celery which has simmered for ten minutes in $\frac{1}{2}$ pint of cream. Serve with cubes of bread fried in bacon fat. (One serving of this celery soup is sufficient to feed the average British pig for one ninth of a day.)

Celery Hotpot for 1
2oz calf's liver in strips, 1 lamb's kidney, sliced and 3oz rump steak, cut into 6 cubes, are marinated in a glass of red wine and a tablespoon of sunflower oil, for at least 12 hours. Add a

88

medium-sized raw potato, diced, and half a dozen each pickling onions and button mushrooms. Bake in a closed oven dish in a medium oven for 50 minutes and just before serving ladle off excess fat and stir in half a gill of double cream boiled up with a little cayenne pepper. Celery is optional.

Celery Trifle for hardly anyone
This is an old Cumberland recipe in which you substitute celery for custard; it is recommended by old Cumbrians.

Until the middle of the nineteenth century, cookery books dealt with medicine as well as food and it is the medicinal aspect of celery which will, I think, interest readers and gives celery its deservedly unique place in horticulture. There are households in and around the celery fields of Prickwillow that already appreciate the wide range of celeremedies, but this is, I am fairly certain, the first time such a collection has been gathered and presented to a wider public.

Headaches
Cut the green leaves from 4 or 5 celery stalks, chop them, lay them in a heat-proof bowl and add 10 fluid ounces of boiling water. Strain the liquor into a cup and take 3 aspirins. (For children use more celery and less aspirin.)

Constipation
Use the white part of the celery; also Ex-Lax.

Diarrhoea
As above. No Ex-Lax.

Whooping Cough and Kidney Stones
There is no connection between these two ailments and it is presumptious to look for a celery-orientated cure. Go to an antique shop or fish market.

Anorexia Nervosa
Large quantities of celery eaten at regular intervals have been found beneficial here.

Hallucinations
Celery induces hallucinations only when liquidised in a high-speed food processor and mixed with LSD.

Piles
There is a celery-based remedy for these but the disease has been found to be preferable to it.

Birth Control
Take one stick of celery simmered in white wine drained and served with Hollandaise sauce nightly. Avoid intercourse.

Bronchial Complaints
Use the blunt end of a stalk to apply Vick's Vapour. Rub liberally to your chest.

Falling Hair
You can pick these up with a stick of celery moistened with syrup.

SMOKING

When you spat they fined you a fiver
It was once just as simple as that
And the same sum of money was asked for
Whatever the volume you spat.

I have little affection for spitters
But at least *they* all knew how it was
From a delicate expectoration
To the contents of most of their jaws.

When they got caught it cost them a fiver
They could pay . . . or be sent to the nick
Which made sense, was a proper deterrent
And above all was fair and was quick.

What I hate about smoke regulations
Is the notice they stick on the wall
NO SMOKING MAXIMUM FINE £50
   which not only does not scan
But is no disincentive at all.

IF YOU SMOKE YOU GET SENT TO THE SALTMINES
Seems to me to have 'siderable charms
or THIS IS A SMOKING COMPARTMENT
LIGHT UP OR WE'LL BREAK BOTH YOUR ARMS.

But 'maximum fine fifty knicker'
(Not a word what the minimum is)
Confuses perplexes and angers
And poses more questions, like . . . viz:

What's the charge for a pipe in a carriage
Containing a high-caste Hindu?
Are cigars more expensive than gaspers?
What price if you puff in the loo?

Can you plead that your eye-sight is faulty
Or the whiff in your hand was a plant?
That the self-lighting fag in your pocket
You mistook for the *plume* de your *tante*?

Are there rebates for all first offenders?
Special discounts for reefers or pot?
It is time that they came to their senses
Either you're smoking—or not.

CHAPTER SIX

Professionals' touches

A magazine called *Monocle*, which is delivered by the dozen to
the housekeeper of the house in which I live, carries in its
current edition an article about the chef proprietor of a restaurant that is booked solidly for dinner for the next six weeks.
The man practises *la nouvelle cuisine*, and he very decently lets
us into the secrets of one of his salads; 'Try it,' advises *Monocle*.
The ingredients include 4 hearts of artichokes fresh; 1 truffle
fresh (can be tinned); 150 grams goose liver; 1 lemon juice.

I shall not try it. I eat my artichokes with mousseline sauce,
my goose liver with thick, freshly-made toast and consider
truffles among the most over-rated and over-priced commodi-
ties to be unavailable anywhere. Furthermore I do not understand 1 lemon juice.

To go back to *Monocle*, it was once a thin and dreary give-
away magazine and has now become voluminous, readable
and staggeringly up-market. Under 'Property' in the classified
section they list only two houses: one is a seventeenth-century
cottage in the Etruscan countryside, the other a two-bedroom
job at La Jolla in Southern California. There is an enigmatic
entry under 'Personal and General' in respect of a garage to
let in SW1. 'Would suit a two-car family,' it states.

But I digress. It is not two-car families who live in garages that I wish to discuss but the *nouvelle cuisine*. The *ancienne cuisine* consisted of meat and fish masked by sauces, soups thickened with flour, vegetables laced with cream or herbs and spiked with grated cheese. The old way was to serve food to hungry folk and have them leave the table satisfied. No more.

La nouvelle cuisine eschews hunger as a reason for eating. Food intake becomes an exercise in aesthetics. A sliver of crayfish, cut from the distaff end, balanced on a single, crinkly, greeny-white lettuce leaf topped with a field mushroom blanched and pressed through a hair-sieve, ideally by an albino virgin. For accompaniment, five matching under-cooked French beans lightly brushed with drawn butter and a suspicion of a small, almost raw, new Pentland Javelin potato.

And God help you if you eat it all up, or eat it too quickly; much time must be spent admiring the colour scheme, appreciating the blend of textures, comparing every aspect of the minuscule offering with the medallion of sheep's brain that was served surrounded by slices of baby beet and quarters of green limes last week.

Nouvelle cuisine is about food as an art form; it is also one of the principal reasons why McDonald's flourish *and* stay open for substantial late-night fried snacks for home-going victims. Mind you, there was much that was wrong with the old order. The determination of caterers to pre-cook and re-heat and the reluctance on the part of British diners to wait for food had a lot to do with it. The economics of bulk purchasing were not unconnected with the general decline in quality either—for when your market man lands a cheap containerload of gammons, there is a great incentive to boil the lot, freeze half of them and make forty-eight giant speculative tins of Ham Mousse with the rest.

A single gammon on the other hand can be lovingly soaked for sixty hours, the water changed at regular intervals, then simmered and skinned and crumbed and carved—to be served cold with fresh granary bread and mustard butter, or hot with a sauce made by boiling together double cream and dry white wine to which you add an abundance of rough chopped parsley.

Our gastronomy was built on the assembly process. 'Take a basinful of cooked rice,' proclaimed the pundits. 'Add half a basin of chopped roast pheasant and a pint of rich brown sauce. Mix well, fill into a buttered oven dish and bake until piping hot.' There is no place for Pheasant Kedgeree in the new order. Today you select the plumpest section of the pheasant's breast and simmer it in *beurre blanc*. The accompanying rice is poached and dried and shaped to resemble a pheasant egg while a cunningly-cut leek, simmered in veal stock, hovers in attendance. That is the way of it and try not to think of how many chefs' hands were involved in manipulating the contents of the plate into the most favoured position.

Now somewhere between their way and ours there must be a better way and that will be the real break-through. While we leave it to the professionals to discover it, we must put ourselves into the sort of peak condition in which we shall be able to recognise it when it comes. Quite soon now the social gurus who try to influence our tastes and the governmental demons who succeed in picking our pockets will combine to talk us into a glorious state of abstinence.

Prepare for this with large drafts of good wine drunk from large bottles and, before going forth to man the barricades, a light meal of roasted leg of pork with brandied apple sauce and bubble and squeak and baked parsnips could be helpful.

During the war I took lodgings behind the Dorchester Hotel, in which hostelry I served my apprenticeship. The address was 39a Charles Street, London W1, and, despite the quality of the surrounding district, the rent was very low because the building was constructed of wood and incendiary bombs fell nightly upon central London. The rent was cheaper still because 39a was diagonally opposite a pub, and you know how it is with pubs and noise.

I had been in residence for a week when the publican complained about the noise for the first time; it would have to stop, he said. His customers were complaining, and they went on complaining until I left Mayfair to go and make more noise in the Army.

The pub in question was the Red Lion in Waverton Street and while I prefer pubs that have zoological rather than heraldic names (I like the Brown Cow better than the Green Bear), the Red Lion had much going for it in those far-off years when it was commanded by an angry, bloody-minded old patriot called Monty.

Monty was what was then known as a 'man of the old school', though I doubt that school had taken up much of his youth. He ran the place with a fist of iron, telling his customers exactly what it was they could do and especially what they could not do—often using the ultimate sanction available to war-time landlords: the withholding of drink 'due to shortage of supplies'. He also rewarded those who behaved with style by letting them purchase the odd bottle of booze, an almost unheard of war-time rarity.

I did not go back to the Red Lion when I came out of the Army. I had been a Mess Officer for a while and realised, retrospectively, what awful customers I and my friends must have been. Ashamed, I suppose, you would call it.

Last week I received a hand-out from a PR firm stating that the Red Lion in Waverton Street was re-opening after several weeks of refurbishing and that there were now *twelve* different pâtés available at the bar for the delectation of customers, one of which would be the pâté of the week—or the day, I suppose, if one ate enough of it.

Monty would never have sold pâté—a slap round the ear-hole with a slice of Spam was about the extent of his catering—but as it was the Red Lion and I had not been back, I went.

The landlord is now called David and a very different kind of specimen, though with Monty-like politics, I should not wonder. Where Monty was at best a gent, David is a full-blown gentleman. When roused, Monty would shout and throw things. David, were one foolish enough to rouse him, would be menacing in his silence, but what they have in common is they both run/ran a good pub, which in these days, when being a publican seems the mid-term occupation for mini-cab drivers on the road to being property tycoons, is rare. The Red Lion is not only a good pub, it also runs a decent restaurant in which people do not whisper, even though the tables are far enough apart to make whispering unnecessary had it been your intention to go to a place for a private chat.

And the pâtés are there, and are twelve, and anyone who knows about such things will tell you that the larger the variety, the poorer tends to be the quality (read Fosdyke on cheese-trays, 1954).

David's pâtés are not poor, though there were a few I did not much care for, and some of them *sound* terrific, like one constructed of hare, venison, pheasant and Spey Royal whisky; it is only after eating it that you realise it needs belly of pork and bacon and pork fat to give it body which can then be flavoured with game. What you have is sort of game squared, shot with garlic to show there is no ill-feeling.

I picked at terrine of courgette, toyed with taramasalata, admired the marbling of the salmon mousse, and said that chicken liver and I got on about as well as Imperial Leather toilet soap and I. I told him I could take or leave kipper Britannic and then it came.

In the overall list of historic encounters I expect Bertie stumbling across Jeeves, Romeo catching his first glimpse of Juliet, Marshall meeting Snelgrove will all have the edge on my tasting what was marked as Pâté No. 9 at the Red Lion, but Mr David Butterfield's Old English potted beef meets C. Freud, MP, nevertheless deserves a place in that chronicle.

On the hand-out it is simply described as 'Topside of beef pounded with marrowbone stock, mace, garlic and port'. I do not suppose it is any more than that but it is supremely succulent, conjuring up the joy that never came from the millions of jars of meat-paste that one consumed in growing up.

Here at last was a meat-paste worthy of its name, a confection to make the entire Shippam Empire blush. Topside of beef, pounded with marrowbone stock, it said on the menu; and I am sure they are right.

It would be advisable to stand back a bit because pounding together meat and stock tends to splash all who stand and wait; mace and garlic and port are in these somewhere, pounded, I shouldn't wonder, with a mortar and pestle, if one is obtainable.

For my taste there might have been a touch too much garlic, but the meat-coloured mass, topped with clarified butter, served on a generous number of slices of thickly cut, freshly grilled toast with an accompaniment of dairy butter and a bottle of decent Moulin à Vent (which costs nearly £12 at which it is no sort of bargain) could be the very best way of preparing the metropolitan appetite for an evening at the theatre, cinema or wherever it is that *Punch* readers go when the spring sun descends behind the White City stadium.

Good to come home to, afterwards, as well.

To the question 'Do you cook?' I consider the answer 'No, I buy' to be perfectly acceptable.

There is absolutely nothing clever about going to a shop, purchasing a raw chicken, taking it home, thawing it, and rubbing it with fat and salt prior to cooking it for its allotted time when you could have gone to another shop, or the cooked food counter of the same establishment, and bought a roast chicken. (You re-heat a roasted bird by wrapping it loosely in well-buttered foil and leaving it in a medium hot oven for about twenty minutes.)

And making pâté is only smart if what you make is significantly better or cheaper than what you can buy. Soups that come out of tins are never so totally disgusting that they cannot form a basis of something pretty good. Baking your own bread is therapeutic, but the end product is seldom better, never cheaper than the bread you buy in a small baker's shop.

If you do not enjoy cooking and accept the economists' argument that you must add the cost of your time to the price of the ingredients (everyone can make 8op an hour addressing envelopes or taking in washing), a carefully bought meal is likely to be neither much worse nor any more expensive than one of your own creation. Here is a menu:

Vichyssoise: buy a tin. Buy a quarter pint of double cream. Put soup and cream into a blender, add six ice cubes and blend until ice stops rattling. Serve very cold with chopped chives (buy these) and coarse salt.

Pâté: buy the best that you can find. Buy good butter and serve this in a slab. Garnish with radishes and watercress. Buy fresh wholemeal loaves (sprinkle them with water and give them ten minutes in a hot oven if you want people to think that you baked them yourself). Pour the contents of a bottle of Escoffier Cumberland Sauce into a sauce boat; it is a sensational accompaniment.

Pasta: buy a packet of whatever shape most appeals to you. You boil pasta for exactly the length of time it says on the packet. (If you can boil water you can boil pasta.) In another pan (sorry about this; you will feel like Fanny Cradock having all those pans on the go at one time), you decant a quarter pint of single cream, a small tub of Parmesan cheese, and a slice of ham cut into small scraps, and heat to the point where it bubbles. Then cut off the heat. Add garlic salt if you like garlic. When pasta is cooked, drain it in a sieve, decant into a heated bowl and anoint with the contents of the other pan. People will cheer and hail you as a maestro, which allows you to serve:

Fishcakes, which you buy; the better the food shop, the better the fishcakes are likely to be. Wrap in well-buttered foil, heat in oven till very hot (say, 15 minutes on Mark 5 which is 375°F) and serve with interesting chutneys and a tomato salad with dressing which comes in bottles. You *will* have to cut the tomatoes into slices or quarters.

Cheese is something about which I will not have to tell you, other than that English matured farmhouse cheeses are excellent and worth the money.

Ice-cream is sold in packets, many of which are better than some, and you can now buy ice-cream sauces like fudge sauce, chocolate marshmallow sauce, etc. If you want to use a saucepan again, wash the one that held the cream/garlic/ham and cheese and put into it two tablespoons of milk, two of water and two Mars bars cut into small pieces. Stir while this heats up over a low flame and the 'sauce' becomes tacky and desirable; it goes amazingly well with good vanilla ice cream over which you pour the bubbling mixture just before it burns. You may have to try this out once or twice.

Coffee involves boiling water again. There is no good reason why you should not use the same receptacle as you did for the pasta though there are some who swear that aqua from a kettle has special qualities.

There will come a time when your reputation as a master chef might embarrass you to the extent of wishing to achieve something on your own. Try personalised rolls. Scotch baps are best but any bread roll with a smooth top will do; miniature Hovis is all right also.

Let us suppose you have as a guest someone called Peter— or Pauline. You take a pair of nail scissors and cut from the front page of a magazine the letter 'P'. Place this in the middle of the roll or mini-loaf. Engage a pastry or paint brush in the cream at the top of a bottle of milk and paint all over the whole surface of the roll. Bake for five minutes in the top of a medium oven and then remove the letter from the bread. The 'P' stands out remarkably. For people called Xenobia, Butch or Atalanta, take similar action with the appropriate letters.

There was in a magazine a picture of a slice of terrine and a dish of chutney and some rounds of French bread; also a saucer of pickled onions and gherkins. The author told you in several hundred well-chosen words about marinating pieces of chicken liver overnight in a blend of Armagnac and sherry, brown sugar and crushed peppercorns, and gave details of the sized cube into which you cut belly of pork (quarter-inch, she said, and told you in centimetres in case you were a Eurofreak) and the way in which you cooked the stuff and cooled it and waited a bit and then weighed it down with a light weight—but not until the fat ran clear and the mass came away from the sides of the dish. It looked very good in the magazine; *très nouvelle cuisine*, as we say in the trade.

What she did not tell you was that in France, where the pâté came from, few right-minded people would think of preparing such a dish. They would call their chauffeur and request that he went to the charcuterie and obtained, in exchange for some insignificant number of devalued francs, whatever quantity of the chicken liver terrine in Armagnac was required for the meal in question.

Imperceptibly—unless you were especially looking out for it—there has built up in Britain a cottage industry of pâté-makers: women, perhaps ladies would be more accurate, who entered matrimony with not much more than a certificate from Prue Leith, Tante Marie, Oncle Carrier or their local Poly's home economics department; they now spend the nights marinating and the days chopping and cubing and finding plates of the right weight to make just what it was that the magazine would have you produce—only they do it better because they spend more time at it, and have more experience, and their husbands beat them if they do not eke out the housekeeping allowance with the revenue from their handiwork. The trouble is, we do not consider it proper not to cook for our guests.

In France, the serving of shop-bought cooked food is generally accepted; 'We shall go and eat at the Dubois; they have a superb patissier and a brilliant boucherie that prepares quenelles,' people say, without a word of criticism about the Dubois not staying up all night and spinning sugar for the candied pineapple which you will be given for pudding. In England, and I dare say in Scotland and Wales as well, you have to go to some lengths to pretend that the produce you buy from the local shop, or wherever it is that the good women sell their stuff, is yours and has caused you the requisite amount of production misery.

Local potteries are a good answer. Go and find out which of the available terrines are most to your liking, and have pots made to fit them; ask the potter to make the dish in your favourite colour and affix to it a crest with your initials. Then buy what you like and decant into what is yours. There is no chutney which, refreshed with garlic vinegar and a dash of brandy and a spoonful of ginger marmalade, will not taste like an exclusive creation.

Nouvelle cuisine or not, I did not care for the clinically cut rounds of French bread; splash the bread with water, stick it into an oven for a few minutes and tear it for your guests. Use a butter mould to make a good impression upon a packet of Anchor butter and serve with this a few radishes washed and tailed and slightly—but not completely—topped. Sea salt is important with radishes. So much for a starter.

Salmon is available in the shops and while Scotch salmon and pink trout are expensive, Canadian frozen salmon is not much dearer than fresh cod or haddock and can be made delicious (as can fresh cod and haddock) but also expensive-looking, which is hard to do with plebeian fish. The secret of salmon is not so much the broth in which you cook it as the liquor in which it cools and which it assimilates.

Prepare a little court bouillon made of equal parts white wine and water with a dash of vinegar. Reduce this by boiling with an onion cut into thin rings, a dozen peppercorns, a red dried chilli and bay leaf or two small ones. Put your salmon into cold salted water, bring slowly to the boil and as the first bubble breaks through the water, decant the fish into a glass serving-dish and pour over it the boiling court bouillon. Allow to cool and serve with your own mayonnaise made by mixing two tablespoons Hellmann's mayonnaise to a coffeespoon of chopped anchovy fillet; garnish with freshly-chopped chives and listen to the compliments.

American restaurants all over London serve pumpkin pie, all of which taste like every other pumpkin pie in London, while they all promise that it is their own. If your powers of detection do not get you to the source, you might just have to buy such a pie from Coconut Grove, Grunt's in Maiden Lane, the Lone Star Café or the Chicago Pizza Pie Factory; it is a sensational pudding benefitting from an application of whipped cream, which should be cold as the pie must be hot.

Most of us have to wait until new potatoes have managed to come to the shops at prices that do not reflect air mail postage from Madeira. Scrub them (do not waste time scraping them) and boil them in salt water until barely cooked. Then put them in a closed pan with quite a lot of butter and a huge amount of rough-chopped parsley and that is the 'cooking' contribution to the meal. You scrub the potatoes the night before, boil them while you eat the pâté, add butter and parsley before you bring in the salmon plates and keep them sizzling while whoever is in charge of the white wine that goes with salmon fills the glasses.

Today's good host-person is the one who lives near the good shops and has the organising/deceiving ability that goes with the heady life punctuated by Falkland Island news flashes. That is our lot.

If you look up 'party' in a dictionary, you will find that it is 'an event where hospitality is dispensed by a host or hosts with the general aim of amusing, sustaining or otherwise entertaining guests'. I used to argue that for this reason bottle parties were occasions to shun. The concept of bringing drink which would be consumed by others—while you took pot luck with theirs—is such a rotten incentive for party-going, such a poor reason for staying away from the pub, that with the alternative of a bottle party or nothing, you should plump for the latter.

(At the end of my bottle-party-going days I would take along a candle and a bottle of whisky, insert one into the other, then light it. Strangely no one ever suspects that there is anything in a bottle beneath a lighted candle.) When you reach the age of forty people stop asking you to bottle parties, so all this may be out of date—I write from distant memory—but with the price of drink at its current level, geriatric events of that ilk may soon be the norm.

What I do find is that while drink at parties is only fractionally nastier than it was (one of the few constructive benefits of EEC membership to date), food has deteriorated quite astonishingly. I remember parties at which there were stews; I have had nourishing party-soups replete with pearl barley and hunks of ham. Risottos of chicken and lobster, kedgerees containing haddock, even pheasant, all abounded on the scene before someone, somewhere, stipulated that the criterion for food at parties must be forklessness; if you can't take it up in your fingers, said the apostle, don't serve it.

102

So there came the age of the cocktail canapé; the chip and the peanut, once a devilish device to make people drink more in bars, was suddenly introduced into the home. Gherkins, an abomination if ever there was one, achieved respectability.

There were bridge rolls filled with not very much and toasted snippets (which would have been better fried in olive oil) made soggy with minced yuk. In the 1950s green asparagus wrapped in thinly-sliced gently-buttered brown bread was invented and the party-machine took it up. We now get tinned asparagus in pre-sliced margarined Hovis, all soggy and squelching in its own saline.

Ring up a professional caterer and his main ambition is to make it quite clear to all that the food which is served could not have been produced by the hostess herself. So the food is hot: chicken livers wrapped in bacon; bits of fried Dublin Bay prawn; anything that you can make a jab at with a cocktail stick. When the caterer is a lovely amateur lady such as one qualified from the Cordon Bleu or Madame Leith, you get a quiche and a dip. And because you need a fork for one and a spoon for the other, quiches are cut into tiny pieces and dips come with nasty Ritz biscuits.

What has happened to sausages then? Remember, the size of the sausage is wholly dependant on the thickness of the gut and the frequency with which knots are tied therein. Sausages used to be made of pork and pork fat and pounded blade mace and mustard seed. They were bound with good rusk in small quantities and cooked slowly so that the unpricked casing or skin did not burst and the taste remained in the sausage instead of escaping into the griddlepan. Today's sausage contains cereal and meat, in that order it often seems, with water and flavouring, colouring, preservatives and taste stimulants, and it is the proud boast of the manufacturers that they have never offended anyone with their wares, not ever.

Let me tell you about the very best sausage in the world. Meat and liquid do not mix readily, not even when the flesh is minced, but if the beast is so freshly killed that the carcase is still warm, you can actually watch the liquid disappear into the meat. So you kill a piglet and immediately cut off one leg and one third of that quantity of hard back fat and mince it. To 4lb of warm minced pork and fat add one pint of champagne, and season the mass with freshly-ground white peppercorns; bind with beaten egg-yolk—that is the mixture. Fill it loosely into casings, remembering that the stuff will expand while it is cooking, then brush the sausages with butter and grill them very gently under as low a grill as will let them cook without causing them to burst (try it with one). If you want to reheat such a delicacy, a small glass of champagne and a pat of butter are simmered together in a dish and the sausages are put therein in the bottom of a slow oven and shaken now and then.

But if you, like me, are sick of run-of-the-mill party snacks and currently unable to find freshly-killed piglets, you may be taken by a salad which I recently made for a coach party of thirty-four. The main advantages were that the total cost was well under a fiver and there was enough for all to have quite a lot each. For the record, it required forks and plates.

14 pounds of new potatoes; 3 ham hocks at Tesco were 70p each—and they sold tinned pickled cucumbers from Roumania at 40p a large tin. I got two. Boiled and peeled and sliced the potatoes. Sliced the cucumbers. Boiled and removed excess fat and bone and skin from the hocks and still had nearly three pounds of meat, which I chopped, not very small. I also thinly sliced three large onions. With the rest of the money I made a mayonnaise using a litre of salad oil, three egg-yolks, lemon juice, mustard, etc., and added it to the salad ingredients which I had first mixed with the stiffly-beaten whites of the three eggs. That stops the potatoes from 'drinking in' the mayonnaise.

It is the sort of food that would make me take the candle out of my whisky, if anyone invited me to a bottle party.

Walton and Hersham Football Club, which only a few years ago played so courageously in the FA Cup, is in the hands of the receiver. The bailiffs have moved in and taken away the equipment: boots, goal-posts, balls and embrocation.

I do not want to discuss the merits of the seizure, though on the face of it (bearing in mind the second-hand value of a football boot, let alone partially-used bottles of Sloan's liniment) it sounds as if there was an element of spite about the operation. I mean it is a bit like taking a cork-screw from a bankrupt wine-butler or depriving a fallen prostitute of her bed linen.

How will Walton and Hersham stage a come-back—naked, bare-foot, on a field bereft of uprights, cross-bars or nets? On reflection, that is probably how they *will* make a come-back— for while I have never been to Hersham and remember little of my few visits to Walton, most people would make something of an effort to witness eleven nudists cruising around on a ball-less, goal-less pitch.

The reason why the demise of Walton and Hersham Association Football Club made the news is, of course, the rarity of such events. By and large football clubs do not close; public-spirited men beset by nostalgia and the hope of official recognition step in wielding a cheque book and Papermate.

Had the receiver moved into a restaurant, no one would have bothered to commit the occurrence to print, unless it had opened the month before with a huge flourish. People think back upon the football matches of their youth with tears in their eyes: 'Those were the days; they don't make players like that any more; Dixie Dean would be worth seven Kevin Keegans with two Ray Clemences thrown in as makeweight'— but the meals of yesteryear were rubbish. What folk recall is the atmosphere, the waitress with the cleavage, the time your knee touched Diana's while the Welsh rarebit was served, and if you should think back upon a particular dish, there's not much point in saving the place from the brokers' men, not ten years after they transferred the chef.

There are two good reasons why bailiffs tend not to raid larders and cellars: firstly, because new people seem ever eager to take on ownership ('It can't be difficult; our bloody house is like a bloody restaurant; I might as well get paid for the hospitality'); secondly, because of the ease and speed with which one is able to dispose of food and drink before the men with the hard hats make their entrance.

In the spring of 1945 my father, who much enjoyed his food, searched the morning papers for news of European liberations and booked tables in Soho restaurants according to the latest bulletins from the front. Thus did he enter into the brouhaha surrounding the relief of occupied Belgium and Holland, Hungary, Ceechoslovakia, Romania, Poland, all of which national eating houses had put by a few bottles for just this occasion.

As City Editors recommend shares that you should sell, so ought restaurant critics advise their readers where they should soon be able to get a last supper, a farewell do, a positively-everything - must - go - we - are - closing - down - at - midnight - on-Saturday occasion. Why is it that you keep meeting people who say, 'I met you at the opening night of the India,' or 'Why weren't you at the launch of J. B. Brasserie?' You never meet anyone who celebrated the last rites at the Caprice, or the Coq d'Or, or any of the thousands of unsuccessful operations that shut up shop each year.

It can be a great joy for one and all, the last night. The owner has written off his losses; the staff have got their redundancy pay; the police realise that a raid to catch after-hours drinking would be a pointless exercise and the customers wonder whether, if they stop the cheque, there will be anyone to write them Dear Sir Unless letters.

The chef knows that it was his reputation and skill which closed the establishment, so he won't be trying too hard; the dish-washer realises that to break is quicker than to wash; the cashier cannot have great interest in balances, not when she knows that the cash will go into the owner's pocket and the cheques will bounce—and the doorman who parks your car spends the last two weeks at work leaving vehicles on double yellow lines and removing the parking tickets.

But there are last nights, like that at the Gavroche before they moved to their newer, bigger, more charismatic premises, which are exceptions to the rule. These are last nights caused by success and very rare events they are. Perhaps the best we can do is to cash in on temporary closures. The *Guide Michelin* tells you that this or that place is open from March to the last week in October. The last day of that last week is a date to enter in your diary; I have had some marvellous hospitality when the alternatives were us—or the pig-bin.

It could well be that I am overly suspicious, but I have never trusted Michelin maps any more than I would put my faith in Burberry's weather forecasts or a Health Chart produced by a tobacco company. In the case of Michelin, whose prosperity depends on people driving the maximum mileage on their excellent tyres, is it not suspect when they go to such lengths to let you in on short-cuts?

However, when it comes to the food guides which the company publishes, there is no conflict and I have long admired the French edition and have even derived some small happiness using those in respect of Spain and Italy. I am less enthusiastic about their British book, because they judge what we do from the point of view of classic French gastronomy. They classify with the minds of Franco-professionals, which means that the food which 85 per cent of Britons like best—and about 3 per cent of our restaurants do very well—will hardly be considered, let alone deemed worthy of a star for excellence. (When it comes to stars, *Michelin GB* is like Madame Tussaud's Planetarium during a power cut, though they drop one in the direction of Tiger Lee's Chinese emporium in Old Brompton Road.)

In France, the *Guide* occasionally leads you to a centre of regional excellence like a tripe parlour in Normandy. In Britain, the criterion is how close you can get to the fare of the Widow Point, the Brothers Troisgros or Father Bocuse; no hope there for a brilliant fish-and-chip shop or the best Devon cream tea-rooms.

Every year, in spring time, the guides come out with their new annual assessments and the gastro-scribes are invited to come and eat and drink and collect their free copies. The norm has been for this event to be held in an establishment which has been particularly commended in the small print and the scribes have the opportunity to re-assess the food at the launch and agree with the quality of the criticism.

107

Michelin did not do that. They gave a launch at their offices and asked a caterer to come in and do the food. I went, sort of agog. We arrived. There was much wine, also the men from the *Financial Times* and *The Observer* and the BBC and the lady from the *New Standard* and someone who had got hold of someone else's invitation and probably worked on the Pets Wanted column, but came regardless; I recognised also a few other familiar faces.

What did they give us, do I hear you ask?

The sort of food which would not have got a star, not anywhere, ever. A rather dull brawn of fish, flakes of this and that set in gelatin with a sauce that was quite pleasant but would not have made you look up. Some jolly nice boned rolled lamb with an acceptable sauce and mashed carrots and mashed celeriac (which had somehow come out green) and then an orange-flavoured junket with slices of real orange, followed by cheese (Brie and Stilton) and coffee. Ah well.

We sat discussing this and that and a bistro called Anna's Place which is only open at night, closes for weeks on end several times a year and is so full that you have to book a month ahead. One of our number said that she went there all the time. I am all for places that are so full that you cannot go there; I wish the guides would say 'pointless to book' instead of 'essential to book'.

In France, if a restaurant is not in the *Guide*, you *know* it is either very new or it isn't worth a visit. In Britain you have a sneaking suspicion that they missed it, the way they missed The Falcon at Whittlesey or the White Lion Hotel in Wisbech, to name only the first two places I looked up.

A guide, it was thought, cannot be really nasty about a restaurant for fear of libel action, though the Chinese place in New York which was slated in *The New York Times* and sued the paper for a million dollars has not had an empty table since the critique was published. New Yorkers stand in line to see for themselves whether the food is as foul, dirty, inedible, cold, flavourless and unauthentic as the critic stated.

This does not surprise me and British gastro-guides should have no reason to fear legal action by places they have denigrated because, being the masochists we are, there is no writer who can put people off going anywhere. In France, a whisper to the effect that so and so is not as good as it was, is immensely damaging. In England, you can announce at a cocktail party that yesterday you ate the worst meal you have ever eaten, tell the assembled company where you ate it and why it was so bad and you will spend the rest of the evening telling people how to get there so that they can try for themselves.

Politically I have doubted the accuracy of the contention that no publicity is bad publicity as long as they spell your name correctly. In the field of food and wine I would say it is totally true, which gives even less cause for Michelin and Ronay *et al* to miss out any conurbation.

Let me end with one criticism: when I worked for the *Queen* magazine we had an image of our reader. She was called Caroline and we knew all about her: her age, tastes, habits, state of affluence, and so on. *Michelin GB*, it seems to me, is principally intended for visiting Frenchmen. I just wish that somewhere in the introduction they would say so. If they can tell us a little about their inspectors, that would also help.

Let me remind readers that you do get quite the best food, service, even discount on your bill, if you can make restaurants think you are The Inspector for someone who intends to publish an assessment. There is a lot of benefit and good clean fun for the small inconvenience of stopping every now and then to scribble something on a piece of paper discreetly (though not too discreetly) tucked beneath your bread plate.

I think it is the firm of Laurent Perrier—though it could just be some other French company that does not send me any champagne at Christmas either—which is sponsoring a prize to the person who does most for Anglo-French relations. I have seen the press hand-out and the winner can come from the field of journalism, gastronomy, travel, sheep-strangling, even politics.

I suppose, before long, there will come an announcement from Mother's Pride or possibly Babycham about a substantial crock of gold to the individual who does least for the cordiality of the old entente and that would be an altogether more amusing competition for which to enter. Of late, I could not help noticing that London hotel restaurants, jealously regarding the prosperity of the French family-Sunday-lunch-out, are doing their damnedest to get in on the action. These restaurants, because hotels do tend to retain the odd customer on the seventh day, have got to open their dining room doors and because Sunday residents are a dying breed, most of whom are asked out to private houses anyway, the management is forced to look elsewhere for trade.

In France they do not have to look far: it is *la famille*, replete with *les enfants*, *le chien*, not to mention *grand-mère*, who fill the tables. As *les chiens* bark and do ugly things to *le tapis*, it was clearly undesirable to provide dog-orientated meals. So, the way to a rich man's stomach not being via his four-legged friend, and grandma is the thin end of the wedge, that leaves the children.

In France, children sit quietly, contemplatively, behind large napkins tied around their necks and not tied nearly tightly enough. To French children gastronomy is as serious a subject as religion and while they sip wine diluted with mineral water they tuck into calf's head about which they are wise. In view of that, it must have sounded impressive to the hoteliers when their public relations consultants came up with the grand idea that *le business* would flourish if parents were given a special incentive to bring kids—like 'half-price and all you can eat from the sweet trolley'.

Now there are a number of subjects about which I am less than tremendously knowledgeable, but British youth and gastronomy are not among them. Therefore, before any friendly caterer jumps on that particular bandwagon and considers offering reduced price meals to juveniles, let me tell him from experience: the ideal Sunday lunch *en famille* is one from which children are removed and granny is best slipped a large glug of Polish Pure Spirit in her Saturday night Horlicks. If an English restaurateur wants to attempt to recapture the French scene, let him emigrate—and thereby become eligible for the

Laurent Perrier, or possibly the Mother's Pride, award.

But there *is* money in feeding kids, separately. Parents will pay large sums of hard-earned, heavily-taxed cash if it appears as if they were taking the children out, just so long as they do not have to sit with them and tell them to keep quiet and not do that, definitely not this, let alone the other. The first establishment that serves reasonable tuck to parents and provides a separate enclosure for their offspring, is going to cash in.

The kids' room must be large and clean with one wall showing continuous noisy cartoon films and the floor should be hard because when accidents happen they should not be trivial. By way of staff, make the ratio one to twelve and recruit from the ranks of sergeant-majors of the Brigade of Guards and ex-Holloway prison officerettes. Drink is unimportant as long as it is fizzy, there is a variety of colours, you provide lots of ice cubes and at least four straws per person. Let the tables be strewn with salty biscuits in packets and sachets of tomato sauce and mayonnaise and envelopes of salt and sugar and pepper, also mini tubes of mustard.

You then give them bags of crisps, all flavours from plain salted to newt and watercress; also bowls of peanuts and sultanas and pieces of cucumber. For the main dish, sausages and chicken legs and fish fingers and hard-boiled eggs are all right if there is a constant flow of hot fresh chips. For puddings ice-cream will do. Let them have toffee apples and Smarties and Liquorice Allsorts and quite a lot of damp soft cloths.

None of the ingredients cost a lot of money and when it comes to charging I would propose £3.50 for the first hour and £2 an hour after that. The staff will be entitled to impose penalties for particularly foul behaviour, as an alternative to which you could agree to allow them to beat your children for a small discount; that would certainly make the recruitment of personnel easier.

CHAPTER SEVEN

Round the clock

Monsieur Brillat-Savarin wrote: 'Tell me what a man eats and I will tell you what he is.' He was referring to Frenchmen.

A gastonome and sage (human, not herbal) he held, not unnaturally, that if a man ate truffles baked in puff pastry, followed by salmon trout garnished with sorrel and veiled with a sauce fashioned of Saumur and cream, he was an altogether better fellow than the one who sluiced down potato soup interrupted by cubes of salt pork.

Good thinking, that.

The reason why the Sage is now largely forgotten (though I shall always remember his 'Oh, sons of Eden who ruined it all for an apple; what might you not have done for a young duckling stuffed with a perfumed forcemeat?') is, firstly, that his assertion made no provision for socio-economic classes; secondly, that in these days of instant convenience foods it no longer applies.

Now if he had opined: 'Tell me when a man drinks and I'll tell you where he is,' he would not only have been on to a good thing; his name would have remained as readily on our lips as Rodney Marsh or John Stonehouse.

If the reply were 'from 6.30 a.m. until 3 a.m.' the complete imbiber would instantly be placed as a Frenchman or Italian (after all, the barman has to sleep some time and Le Patron requires *quelques heures* to count the takings.)

From 5.30 p.m. to 6.15 p.m. would place the victim in the Antipodes where for many years they believed that the shorter the time that a bar stayed open, the less people would drink. When they discovered this to be false, that far from regulating the alcoholic intake, Australian opening hours simply raised the drunks' speed of knocking back booze—the authorities radically reformed the drink laws and you can now stay drinking in Sydney deep into the wee small hours . . . like 7.15 p.m.

'When it is dark' would have persuaded Brillat that he was with an American. When Prohibition ended, tavern owners realised that the only way to keep up the high sales of liquor was to simulate the secrecy of those glorious dry years and they bought heavy curtains and pretended that the whole thing was still on the shady side of justice.

The regulation of drinking hours is peculiarly British in origin and concept. The endearingly simplistic belief that a man is kept on the straight and narrow by being denied opportunity of sin, remains with us still—and accounts for the huge number of drunks as well as a substantial volume of rapists.

So there we are. With few exceptions you may drink to your throat's content from eleven till two and then again from six to ten . . . with an extra half-hour on Saturday nights, which is clawed back, with interest, on Sundays.

Mind you, just as the Law is an Ass, so are the drinking laws pretty asinine and if you are prepared to wear an overall, go greyhound racing, eat brown bread and butter and check in at a sleazy hotel from three to five in the morning you may gulp for twenty-four hours a day and the ghost of Brendan Behan will salute and call you 'Sorr'.

The timetable would be as follows:

5 a.m. Don some form of protective clothing and go to New Covent Garden where there is a handy licence that allows pubs to serve porters on duty.

10.30 a.m. Covent Garden pubs make way for more general licensed premises.

2 p.m. To shouts of 'It's not the landlord's wish', make your way to an afternoon greyhound race meeting. Watford is particularly unattractive . . . but the bar is open until the last race; only half an hour or a brisk lurch to the nearest pub.
. . . Where you while away the 6 p.m. to 10 p.m. watch.

1o p.m. Go to a club or restaurant that has a late licence (midnight or 2.30 a.m. if they have a band). The law requires that restaurants serve drink only with food at this time of night. Thin brown bread is food. There is no compulsion to eat . . . except for the price they charge.

2.30 to 5 a.m. Is admittedly tricky. For some years at Earls Court they had an annual six-day bicycle race where there was a bar which stayed open while the cyclists pedalled. Someone, somewhere, saw the error of their ways and I am afraid the best chance of remaining topped up now is to book into an hotel that has a night porter.

I am sorry about that . . . but genuine all-night bars, like free milk and a Liberal government, are not currently on offer.

Much fuss is made of English breakfasts; deservedly.

Egg and bacon is one of the great culinary marriages. Toast and butter and marmalade is a serious gentlemanly way to begin the day. Kippers, especially those that emanate from the Isle of Man, simmered in milk and then grilled after an application of butter, wakens your palate like few other dishes and remains within the awareness of your taste-buds well into the afternoon.

The Danes break their fast on bland ham (actually they do nearly everything they do on bland ham), the Germans guzzle early morning cheese, as do the Dutch and the Swiss; Rumanians are into yogurt, Hungarians go for ante-meridian salami . . . and the French start the day with eggy brioche and flaky croissants that crumble on impact and rest upon your tie like an outbreak of edible confetti.

French coffee for all its quality and expertise vested in percolation, is served in large cold cups; the temperature of these beverages rate low in gallic priorities.

In the United States, breakfasts are marshalled in by iced water and end on doughnuts. At some random point in between they show their contempt for civilisation via waffles swathed in maple syrup. In Japan early morning noodles float in an opaque sunrise soup.

No doubt about it; we do it best.

French cafés mount their daily newspapers on sticks so that you can: (a) adjust the distance of your reading material beyond the reach of your arms; (b) not take it with you when you leave the premises; (c) poke a distant waiter should you require his services.

We begin in London with *The Times*, lightly ironed to remove creases and bring the paper to a little above body heat for comfort. After a glance at the Obituary column (if only to ensure the absence of your name) you use the expanse of newsprint as a shield against unwelcome companions who may want to look at you, or even speak. Holding the paper firmly in the left hand you disengage the right and grasp the Irish silver teaspoon (which is pointed) to ease a pig or two from the cold immaculately segmented grapefruit in its Lalaque bowl. No sugar; cinnamon if you desire.

Trendies, one is given to understand, go for Rice Krispies which are now eaten in stereo with speakers strategically placed around the dining room. I am a Grape Nut man and would advise good men to follow this example. Nice quiet cereal, Grape Nuts. I take them straight, with a little black Barbados sugar and a dash of very cold half milk/half cream.

Brennans in the French quarter of New Orleans do a 'special breakfast' which costs a lot of money and involves standing in line till they sort out who sits where.

Included in the set meal is Californian champagne, eggs Benedict, English muffins and a lot of noisy fuss.

As I think I mentioned earlier, we do it best.

Try the Connaught Hotel in Carlos Place, London . . . or, still in London, the Savoy, Claridges, the Charing Cross Hotel —all railway hotels do excellent breakfasts . . . as do most trains. The Midland Hotel in Manchester and Gleneagles in Scotland take breakfasts seriously. The Sherry Netherland in

New York (but actually stateless) would be my trans-Atlantic selection.

For breakfast, then, use fresh eggs ... so fresh that the albumen clings tightly around the yolk and the circumference of the lightly fried egg stretches to no greater expanse than the palm of a Corsican flower arranger (they eat olives and garlic sausage at cock's crow): say a diameter of $3\frac{1}{2}$ to 4 inches.

Of bacon there must be not just a sufficiency but an abundance. It should be streaky rather than the more highly regarded short back. Unfortunately no country in which spare ribs have caught on as a way of life can produce satisfactory streaky bacon.

Fried bread is right. Crisply fried in bland oil, drained on kitchen paper, sprinkled with salt and then slipped under the egg ... a slice for each egg. And the toast must not be too thin and be served in racks. The butter should only be salted if you take relish rather than marmalade and the marmalade (with the unsalted butter) must contain much thinly cut bitter peel and may contain slivers of ginger. Breakfast conversation is confined to monosyllabic grunts among which *shuddor*, *shrup* and *cupsmt* may seem the most apposite.

Breakfast mushrooms must *not* be those small white apologia for edible fungi. Huge, firm, fresh black mushrooms are best; wiped, cut diagonally and simmered in butter with a late dash of lemon juice and a sufficiency of salt and pepper. Serve these with rashers of crisp bacon.

A breakfast sausage contains a little more filler (like rusk) than does the health food shop-type sausage which is 95 per cent meat (you cannot get 100 per cent if you want sausage to stick together). Brush with oil into which you have mixed a little curry powder and a dash of Tabasco. Do not pierce them unless you actually want the goodness to flow into the grill pan. Grill for quite a long time under a low-to-medium grill. There is nothing remotely desirable about underdone sausage. Serve with Gordon's vineyard mustard.

One mass-produced beer, unless you are amazingly perceptive, is so like another that I have been steadily surprised by big breweries spending their promotions kitty on trying to impress on us drinkers the uniqueness of taste, rather than the special benefits, of their products. I would try a beer that promised to cure in-growing toe nails, relieve dandruff, or fight tooth-decay.

To me, and I suspect to many other beer amateurs, it is a matter of complete indifference whether I drink Watney's, Whitbread's, Courage's or Charrington's: all perfectly adequate beers if you care for that sort of thing, but driving along the A-Whatsit to Wherever, you would not say, 'We must stop here, it's a Watney's House'. The beers are all reasonable, cool and fizzier than I like, and have been brewed as a result of careful analysis of the public taste—an analysis that is able to gauge with some accuracy what the public do *not* want.

As a consequence people do not complain about our beers and company chairmen stand up at AGMs to announce that this has been another successful year of entrenchment with complaints down to a new low of one per 49,580 pints. There is no large brewery that would make me stop for a pint of their beer, the way I stop for wares of Paines of St Neots or Adnams of Southwold.

Now Whitbread's have very properly looked at this situation and employed a public relations company to promote pub food in their houses—a jolly wise move, I should have thought, had it not been for what the Cheltenham public relations company, whom they employed, have done. Had it been me, had Whitbread's in their wisdom eschewed Cheltenham and said, 'You, Mr Freud, are just the sort of man to whom we would like to give a million or two to promote our pub food,' I would not have listed every Whitbread pub, in each district.

I would certainly not have written to me and asked me to send 36p in stamps to receive booklets called *Pubfood As You Like It around Stratford-upon-Avon* etc. and enclosed with the letter a booklet on Pubfood in Devon which lists every one of their houses and tries to get all enthusiastic about cold buffets and warm snacks, also drawing attention to the amazing quality of a particular Ploughman's Lunch. (In my part of the country, our ploughmen have semolina pudding for lunch;

117

this is given to them by the good ladies who work in old people's homes.) If Whitbread's had come to me, I should have said: (a) about time too, and (b) if any brewer became connected in the public mind with one item of good and desirable pub food it would do more for their trade than all those jolly telly commercial songs put together.

If I drove down the A-Whatsit and passed a Smither's Pub and knew that Smither's were the ones that always served shepherd's pie made with real shepherd *and* provided good green tomato chutney, I would forgive them their beer and patronise them to the exclusion of Smother's whose houses occasionally had this and that.

The Cheltenham public relations company said that some pub was jolly strong on fish. Had they said which fish, how fresh it was, in which manner they cooked it and what was the accompanying sauce or flavour of vinegar, it might, just might, have made me go to that pub. But if I knew that all the pubs under that banner always had a particular dish, I would stop at such a pub when I had not intended to break my journey.

Pork pies might be a good idea for a pub campaign for at best they are delicious. A colour supplement not so long ago asked Mr Paisley, Lady Di Spencer and an England cricketer, who as a result of what happened in the West Indies had better be nameless, to test-taste some pork pies on behalf of readers. They missed the point (and I probably got the people wrong). Pork pies are OK. What makes them less so is when they have been OK for so long that their acceptability departed before your arrival.

Now if one could invent a self-destructing pie, one with a small, inexpensive, edible fuse that blew itself up 36 hours after manufacture, and a chain of pubs always had those, trade would come hammering at the doors. If destruction seems too radical in thse moderate times in which we live, some system whereby the pie turns green after a given number of hours might be a substitute—though this could adversely affect your digestive tract.

The people in Cheltenham have left a space by each descriptive entry so that pub-crawlers can collect special stamps and stick them in the book—just as if they didn't know that people who collect stamps are not the same people as those who collect public houses.

A special Scotch egg would get them. The trouble about Scotch eggs is that there is too much egg, cooked too hard, encased in sausage of poor quality. Perhaps a pullet's egg, cooked for five minutes, peeled and deep-fried in a wrapping of sausage meat enriched with chopped bacon and spiked with mace, would be the answer. There is on the market some quite excellent mustard made of mustard seed and horseradish. The steady availability of that would make me drink almost any-one's beer.

Baked potatoes in pubs could catch on. They are one of the very few things that are not ruined by a microwave; they can be served with a huge number of excellent accompaniments from butter to soured cream and chives via cheese mixes, anchovy dressings, tomato and garlic paste—and brewers could deliver sacks of Pentland Dells or King Edwards with the beer barrels on a Monday. This would also be a very welcome shot in the arm for our declining potato trade.

On the subject of trade, when I ran my Mepal Liberals Royal Wedding Beer Festival in a marquee on Mr Beane's field, I was able to provide a £1 pack for people who are hungry and don't want to queue. A Kingdom apple; a piece of matured farmhouse cheese, a home-baked bap, a plastic cup and bottle of special Royal Wedding Brew. Why cannot theatres do something like that in the invervals?

You can understand how it came about: the Editor of the *Sunday Express Magazine* looked at the calendar and said, 'The issue of March 14th is the one after the Budget. We'll do a financial feature.'

'Whaddat bawss?' asked his assistant.

'More than ever at this point in time—after the savage mauling perpetrated on the people of Britain by the Chancellor of the Exchequer—readers of this great paper will need to look after such cash as remains . . .'

'Lynch Sir Geoff? Ain't we a Tory paper?'

'Advice,' said the Editor. 'Advice on how to make the bread go round; we'll give them ten ways of saving money.'

'Only ten?'

'All right, twenty.'

And one way and another the figure rose to fifty; damn fine advice some of it, like 'Learn to estimate quantities so that you don't buy $1\frac{3}{4}$lb steak when you only need $1\frac{1}{2}$lb.' Serve kipper fillets with lemon juice in the dark and make people feel it's smoked salmon. Economise by buying Sevruga caviare instead of Beluga (this saves you £56 a pound; for the record they mis-spelt Sevruga). If you travel a lot a light plane is cheaper (they claim that a four-seater costs £32,000 and does fifteen miles to the gallon; true only if you tow the light plane behind a car, and you will be very lucky to find a road wide enough.)

Advice flash No. 34 tells you to use the freezer effectively: freeze stock and usable left-overs. Bake in batches to save fuel and freeze the surplus.

Fourteen hints later, they recommend that you keep your fur coat wrapped in the freezer.

I understand why it should be wrapped; with all that surplus bread and frozen stock around an unwrapped fur coat would become tacky and crumbly in no time—but where exactly do you put it? I mean at the front or the back? Under the ice-cream or on top of it? It seems to me that this gem poses more questions than it answers, though they are right in saying that it saves you Harrods' storage charges and prolongs the life of the coat by fifteen years. They forget to mention that this depends on you and the freezer living that long. Nevertheless, 'My wife is defrosting the silver fox' is a great conversation-stopping line.

But it is item 29 that I wish to discuss in some depth: 'Ask people to tea instead of dinner. Cucumber sandwiches, China tea, cinnamon toast, cake, champagne are flash, but nowhere near as expensive as a three-course dinner . . .'

If the friends of the anonymous author of the *Express Magazine*'s 'Fifty Ways' are like my friends, irrespective of when they arrive, they stay until midnight unless they pass out earlier; if you ask them to tea they are going to stay for dinner. I mean what does a man full of champagne, China tea and cinnamon toast do at 6.15 p.m.? The answer is that he stays exactly where he is and asks for more champagne, then throws up his cinnamon toast.

Far better advice is to ask people to supper, or better still not to ask them at all. Very economical solution that.

But to revert to tea as a means of entertaining: tea is in the rush-hour; tea is when the kids come home from school; tea is when working people work and at weekends when they watch sport on television or listen to God on the radio. Tea-time is a rotten time to drink champagne and China tea is a poor accompaniment to sparkling wine.

What the article totally fails to appreciate is that entertainment is about generosity, and serving things by candlelight in order to deceive, buying cheap when you might buy expensive and serving the right drink at the wrong time is the absolute negation of what party-giving is about.

Entertaining graciously involves being seen to be generous, even wasteful. The one good piece of advice I would give impoverished prospective hosts is to ask fewer people at longer intervals but when they come, give all you can, and to hell with nicely calculated less or more.

One of my sons, who gives parties to which he asks people without actually remembering whom or how many, has sought my advice about the best food . . . bearing in mind that the assembled company may be five or thirty-five. 'Honest, Dad, it couldn't be more than thirty-five.'

Baked potatoes is the answer. The potatoes do not keep very well, but they cost little and everything that makes a potato beautiful can be stored and used over the weeks: butter, sour cream, grated cheese, anchovy fillets, chopped hard-boiled eggs and onions, mayonnaise, mushroom sauce, tomato chutney The spirit of entertainment is encapsulated in the host bringing in two dozen beautifully baked potatoes for three guests.

If you are left with a lot of baked potatoes, scoop the potato from the shell when they are still hot and mix the interior with cream and cheese and keep in the refrigerator (near the fur coat). Keep the shells in a cool place. When required fill the shells with the potato mixture and bake in a medium oven. As for all the butter and cheese and chutney and egg you have left over, why not give a tea party and make sandwiches? Tea parties can be great fun as long as they are not an excuse for *not* giving dinner parties.

Christopher Pease went to Eton, read politics at Exeter University and now lives in a London flat with a fridge and a phone, trading as 'Devonshire Clotted Cream Carriers'. For the record, the last letter of the final word is an exaggeration; the rest of the message is true.

Driving back and forth during his years at Exeter, Christopher noticed that 'Devonshire Clotted Cream Teas' signs diminished as one drove east and became extinct in mid-Somerset. So he set out to discover the source, negotiated a price for five-pound containers and wrote to the managers of hotels which he thought should serve the stuff and did not.

On the morning of his finals he received a letter from the Intercontinental in Park Lane ordering fifty pounds. He wondered whether to take the paper ('I mean, what does a degree matter when your first bunch of enquiries nets a three-figure success?'), got a 2:2 and went into business, or possibly vice versa.

Christopher is now 23 years old, the business has been going eighteen months and while it keeps him off the streets it does not as yet keep him in very much else—which is not as it should be. His best customers are the Davy's chain of City wine bars and the Measures tea-rooms in Windsor, which does go to show that having a merchant banker father and going to Eton is helpful.

We sat over a lemon tea and a black coffee and wondered why Wimbledon did not do clotted cream teas, nor Royal Ascot, Fortnum's, Richoux, Sagne's, Bertaux—come to that, the House of Commons. Why is it that Americans (who buy our smoked salmon and our Stilton) sell as 'cream' sweetened white froth that comes out of an aerosol—into which it should not have bothered to get—when a phone call to 01-352 3373 could have had five-pound cartons of genuine Devonshire Clotted streaming across the Atlantic Ocean, or steaming across—for the shelf-life is a published ten days which means sixteen.

I suppose the answer is a fear of infection, something to do with their hygiene legislation, though with all the ailments that currently abound 'he died of clotted cream' seems to me to have a very much more acceptable ring to it than 'R.I.P. (legionnaire's disease)'. Also, you do not die of clotted cream, it just makes you fat: to be precise, 14 times as fat as a similar quantity of gold top milk and as fat again as whipping cream, for this product of Devon has a fat content of 62.5 per cent (butter is 81 per cent). While we toy with statistics, 'half-cream' has a legal requirement to contain not less than 12 per cent fat which is no great help when you try to teach food technology and mathematics at the same time.

What is so special about this cream is that it enhances pies, puddings and compôtes far beyond the imagination of the mechanic—all right then, cook. What is strange, even unique, is that the sales pattern, when you ignore the huge Christmas peak, is totally un-connected with anything but West-Country tourism.

Devonshire Clotted Cream Carrier hopes to change all that. Just as it was discovered that aficionados of roast pork did not have to burn down pig-sties and lick the embers, so will Christopher Pease enable you to have Devonshire teas without going West.

His motto is 'Stay East. You stand, I will deliver,' and as he sits by his phone (24-hour answering service), he promises that if deliveries are held up, he will drive the 420-mile round trip to lug cartons to the metropolis, as he had to do for the private boxes at Lord's on the Saturday of the Test Match. Shouting, 'The cream must get through,' he arrived at the Members' Entrance at 10 a.m.

If you should be twice blessed, have clotted cream and, in placing it in your refrigerator, notice that the milk has gone sour, then there is nothing for it but a scone binge, for scones are the only sane way of using sour milk; making cream-cheese is more time-consuming, more expensive and less pleasant than buying the stuff from the most plebeian deli.

It is almost impossible to go wrong with the manufacture of scones. For the common or garden variety you need: one pound of flour, which you sieve into a bowl with a level coffee-spoon of salt. Add to this three ounces of margarine or butter (it really does not make much difference) and rub the fat into the flour with your fingertips. Add four level coffee-spoons of baking-powder (half bicarbonate of soda and half cream of tartar if you don't buy mixes) and pour in half a pint of sour milk in a whoosh.

Mix this lightly with a gooden spoon and then knead very, very gently with floured hands. Let the mixture rest for a few minutes, then roll out to a depth of half an inch if you are going to bake it, quarter of an inch if you intend to use griddle or frying pan. The former needs 15 minutes on 375°, which is gas mark 5, or 'quite hot' if you use some other gauge. Cook four minutes on the first side, five minutes on the second if you use griddles or frying-pan sprayed with a very thin film of oil. In olden days the way to do it was to heat the pan and rub it lightly with a piece of suet. The flame under the pan should be low, at about number 3 on a scale of 1 to 10.

If for any reason (and I cannot think of any) you should be displeased with this basic mixture you can add fruit like currants or sultanas; sprinkle in spice such as cinnamon or ginger; sweeten it with sugar, enrich it with beaten egg.

To my taste all this is a huge waste of effort when you have Tiptree's Little Scarlet Strawberry Jam and Devonshire Clotted Cream, though there is a sound argument in favour of eating the jam and cream with a spoon, without accompaniment.

Tea is the drink that goes with this. Good honest Indian tea, with milk from the bottom of a bottle of silver top. You must not overdo the fat content.

Before cookery writers got their own television shows, they were able to write straight cookery books which began with 'Sift 1lb plain flour' and ended 'Bake for 50 minutes in a medium oven.'

They mostly lacked character, which is why one is fonder of the late Marcel Boulestin, who was a precious, enigmatic, chauvinist gastro-literary man, than of Ambrose Heath, who was a competent journeyman cook who could write a bit.

I recently re-read Heath's book, imaginatively entitled *Good Breakfasts*. No introduction, no comments, just chapter after chapter headed successively Cereal, Hot Dishes, Cold Dishes, Fruit, Drink, etc., and thought again that, were it not for the unsociable hour at which they serve breakfast, this, in composition, is by far the most acceptable meal of the day. The running order of fruit, cereal, cold dish, plain hot dish, substantial hot dish is just what one needs around 8.30 in the evening and there will surely come legislation (perhaps via the EEC, who have got to do something sooner or later), whereby dinner is presented at 8.00 a.m. and breakfasts herald the beginning of the night. A good sustaining breakfast is exactly what is needed to get a man through a heavy evening.

Let us forget for the moment about lunch. You start the day with a nice cup of turtle soup, a few lamb cutlets and new potatoes and peas and a bowl of crême brulée; either tea or coffee goes well with this. At night you sit down to the feast. The best breakfast dishes—like galantine of sheep's head and pork cheese, which I take at random from Mr Heath—should be eaten soon after they are made. How the hell do you expect anyone to prepare them for 7.45 a.m. consumption?

I went into Tesco's in Ely and asked for Grape Nuts the other day and the manager said, 'Keep your voice down— Grape Nuts date you.' He is what they used to call 'a caution'.

I have news for him. Like Lyon's tea shops, which are being reincarnated, Grape Nuts are back in metropolitan shops (they will probably reach Ely in the mid-Eighties) and make an admirable first course. Serve them warm, giving a bowl of Grape Nuts five minutes in a medium oven. With Grape Nuts, I should recommend an Alsatian wine of some richness, like a Muscat.

The next course comes with toast. Lots of freshly made, not too thinly-cut brown and white toast. Heath's suggestions are absolutely first-class dishes, though for my taste almost inedible before 12 noon. You make porkcheese by cutting cold roast pork into small cubes; about two-thirds of the cubes should be of lean meat, the rest fat. Use strong pork gravy enriched with red wine, spiked with paprika, thickened with cornflour and boil until thick and aromatic. Pour on to the pork, mix well and leave in a cool place to set, whereafter it is carved like a pâté and can be accompanied by green tomato chutney.

Brawn is good and a bore to make. That used to be the main trouble with breakfast dishes. A decent kedgeree takes an hour or two to make, which is absolutely all right for an evening meal. Alternative dishes that go well with toast are game pâté and kipper mousse.

Eggs come next. Ideally, scrambled eggs; these are much enhanced *not* by draping a tired anchovy fillet over the finished product and calling it a Scotch Woodcock, but by spreading the toast with anchovy butter and then piling on the eggs. The best scrambled eggs contain neither milk nor water. Just honest eggs, mixed with a fork, slopped into a pan of hot but not burning butter and the base of the pan massaged with a wooden spoon every ten seconds, as the mixture sets over the lowest of flames.

You should drink champagne with scrambled eggs. Phonies recommend wines from the Fronsac with brown eggs, Pauillac with free-range whites. Phonies are wrong.

The main breakfast course, which has to give you strength to face the rest of the evening, should contain bacon and mushrooms and sausages and kidneys and grilled tomatoes and also new potatoes, steamed and peeled and sliced and crisply fried in a mixture of oil and butter. Drain well and serve without parsley. With this, a good host serves a selection of three or four different mustards.

The great thing about late-night breakfasts is that you do not have to finish with pudding or savoury as you used to, when you ate dinner. You had some crème brulée for dinner that morning and that will see to your sweet requirements for the day. Finish with a pheasant kedgeree: one cup of chopped pheasant meat, cut from a cold roast bird (you will have to run them over before the shooting season begins) to two cups of rice to one cup of strong brown sauce to half a cup of grated cheese. Put the well-mixed meat, rice and sauce into a heavily buttered oven dish, allow 25 minutes in a medium oven before adding the cheese, turning up the heat and serving the kedgeree when this has formed a tacky crust (about ten minutes). A soft red Burgundy would be what they call an appropriate beverage.

Heath writes a good deal about tea and coffee, suggesting that you go to your merchant and discuss with him which of his blends will go best with your local water. Water, he maintains, is the main reason why some tea and coffee is nastier than others. Thanks to the Water Authorities (whom I have never before thanked for anything), we have certainly come on a treat since those days. Now all the water is equal in taste, so that you can take in the pure quality of Nescafé and teabag.

CHAPTER EIGHT

Round the world

SCOTLAND

In small print, on the backs of the packets of Bertie Bassett's Liquorice Allsorts Selection, they used to relate the legend of how it all began: Mr Bassett, the story went, a fastidious North Country confectioner, ran a shop that steadily got nine out of ten for neatness and prided himself on keeping an immaculate counter. One day, having served a twist of liquorice to one young customer, an ounce of desiccated coconut to another, he perceived a speck of each of these sweetmeats on the mahogany, licked his right forefinger, took up the two morsels and popped them into his mouth.

'Delicious,' he is reported to have said. 'Absolutely blooming delicious.' And in hardly any time at all he had set up a great factory that blew black smoke into the environment while it forged ever more coconut on to ever increasing quantities of liquorice in ever more fanciful shapes.

I found the tale inspiring and was probably one of the few small boys to buy Mr Bassett's products for the literature on his box for I don't much care for liquorice, while dessicated coconut and women wearing Dr Scholl sandals are among my pet hates.

Indeed much of my childhood was spent emulating the rich and successful Bassett and though in our leftish intellectual home there was no mahogany counter, I would pounce on dining-table crumbs like All Bran and bacon rind, parsley and treacle, Christmas pudding and Brussels sprouts ... muttering 'delicious, absolutely, fantastically, amazingly, delicious' and wondering who would put up t'brass for t'factory (or do they call it t'mill, like where there is trubble up at?)

I remembered all this the other evening when I was served an immaculate plate of Cockie Leekie—a classic Scottish soup fashioned of chicken, leeks and prunes. 'How the hell did that marriage come about?' I asked myself—trying to focus on my moustache through the idiot grin engendered by the consumption of half a bottle of Lagavullan, twelve-year-old malt whisky. Was it the Bassett finger syndrome that resulted in specks of boiled chicken, leek and prune being simultaneously consumed in the cause of culinary orderliness? Or could a man really have been quietly supping a chicken and leek broth and said, 'Damn it, this would benefit by a prune or two'? Then again, it might have been a punter intent upon the consumption of an antemeridian plate of prunes who decided that a spot of chicken and leek would do wonders for the compôte?

We shall never know, though I suspect that the real answer comes via the prototype kilted cook who swept chicken and leek into a large pan without noticing the brace of prunes sticking to his hairy forearms; served the lot, and in the cantankerous fashion of those north of the Border insisted on its classicism.

In later years, when one of the egregious innovator's pie-eyed cousins upset a packet of barley into the put, it was just another manifestation of La Cuisine of the Auld Alliance.

Cockie Leekie is now made by boiling a chicken with well-washed, cut-up leeks, removing the grease from the top of the broth and adding a few prunes and a handful of barley.

Of all the rich variety of Scots cookery, nothing has been the subject of more derision than the haggis—which does not contain Harris Tweed. Let me begin by stating that you don't make haggis; you buy it. It is a sheep's paunch, scrubbed inside and out, then stuffed with the boiled, chopped heart and lung, the boiled grated liver, to which is added minced onion, nutmeg, toasted oatmeal, suet, salt, cayenne pepper and white peppercorns.

The paunch is then tied firmly at the open end—bearing in mind that the haggis is sufficiently alive, and cunning, to swell, and must be given room to do so; prick the skin so that the haggis will not explode and simmer him in a good broth for about three hours. Serve with single malt whisky while such members of your entourage as remain sober play 'The Skye Boat Song' on a recorder.

The traditional accompaniment to haggis is mashed turnips or swedes—also kail, sometimes spelt kale (which tastes like billiard-table cloth), but it is the sense of occasion and the drink that are critical.

In Abroath, they cure haddock and these 'tails' of the smoked fillets are a great delicacy. They are baked with cream and butter and salt and pepper as a first course . . . and are even finding favour on the banqueting circuit as Mousse of Smokies —very much more delicate a dish than a kipper mousse.

Herrings, scaled and split and dipped in seasoned oatmeal before being gently fried in butter, are a favourite breakfast dish in the north, but when you write of Scottish fish it is salmon that is supreme: smoked, it is superior to its imitators across the world; fresh, it has a unique flavour, a marvellous consistency and is best eaten with as little culinary distraction as possible; say 'yes' to melted butter or mousseline sauce. Keep Hollandaise and mayonnaise for the potatoes.

There is not room to do more than make passing reference to the excellence of Scots beef and venison and grouse, the profusion and delicacy of their raspberries and loganberries, the variety of their bakers' and confectioners' fares, or the quality of their preserves.

Dundee, known as the town of the three J's (Jute, Jam and Journalism), is reputed to have been the place where a grocer's wife invented marmalade. Dundonians certainly make a wide range of marmalades as well as the rich and famous Dundee cake.

Clootie dumplings are stodgy, syrupy, gingery, fruity cannon-balls which I eat with cream—and they do not. Scots short-bread is delicious—a handsome balance between flour, butter and sugar—and for the genuine formologists, oatcakes as a base to cheese is far superior even to the good range of biscuits from Bath and points south of Hadrian's Wall.

Try the traditional scones: $\frac{1}{2}$lb flour, $2\frac{1}{2}$ ounces butter, a tablespoon of sugar, a bare teaspoon each of bicarbonate and cream of tartar and a good pinch of salt. You rub the butter into the dry ingredients, mix to a stiff dough with milk (or yoghourt), roll out, cut into scone shapes and bake in a very hot oven for about ten minutes.

This is the single most acceptable base for Tiptree's Little Scarlet Strawberry Jam which is the best jam I know.

RUSSIA

If you were to stop the average Westerner in the street and ask him to name the first Russian food that comes to his mind, you would have a fifty per cent chance of getting the reply 'caviare'; the other good answer is 'cabbage'.

This is very typical of the country. In Ireland they tell you: 'If it isn't one thing, it's another.' In the Soviet, if it is not one thing, it tends to be something entirely, diametrically different.

In Britain we have friends, good friends, better friends and best friends. There is no such ascending scale of cordiality in Russia. As Alexandre Dumas wrote, 'If you are not *brate* . . . brother' (and like the Trade Union movement no blood relationship is required) 'or *galoubchik* . . . my little pigeon, you are *dourak* or *soukinsene* . . . terms that I shrink from explaining.'

The Russian cuisine is motivated by its philosophy and its geography. The country lies between east and west, indeed it stretches from one to the other, and the conquests, treaties, pacts and alliances have all played their part in influencing the national taste.

There is a debt to the Prussians, more to the French; Mongols left their mark, as did the Scandinavians and the Asians. You can attend a formal dinner in Leningrad and could be excused for thinking that they had brought a separate chef for each course.

What pervades is *smetana*, sour cream, which is served with the caviare, the soup, the cucumbers, the salted herrings and the stew; also the potatoes with dill (I dare say they rub the strings of the balalaikas with something similar).

My own intake of Russian food has been confined to Intourist hotels, formal Soviet dinners and meals with Russian emigrés, who denied that anything but their own versions were authentic. They denied it loudly and frequently with hugs and slaps on the back and much drink and toast after toast and exhortations to eat more and more—as they shovel food on your plate and leave the dish at your elbow, should you feel hungry.

I found my Russian friends' everyday meals like twinning ceremonies between European towns, only more passionate. I have no reason to believe that outside the Intourist Hotels things are very different.

'Our spirit of hospitality is very strong' is how they put it. You will need strength both in the head and the stomach to cope with its profusion. After the first batch of drinks, certainly before the fourth or fifth, they serve *zanuski* which is Spanish *tapas* and French hors d'oeuvres rolled into one and multiplied.

The humblest house serves a radish or some salt herring, usually both; smoked fish, salami-type sausage, cucumber, marinated mushrooms and hard-boiled eggs with dill. They also serve a dish called Poor Man's Caviare which consists of par-boiled chopped aubergine mixed with chopped, crisply fried onions, tomato paste and olive oil.

It is argued that, in a country in which distances are long, the roads bad and punctuality at a premium, the overture to a meal has no right to be short. Beware of *zanuski*. After several hours thereof (lobster salad, steak Tartare and game pies are not unusual components) comes the dinner. Soup is traditional. The famous *schi*, currently confined to classical literature, prisons and the peasantry, is a mixture of cabbage, sauerkraut and boiled buckwheat, served with black bread.

Borsch: however you decide to spell it, it is the most famous

132

Russian soup but the red beet juice with sour cream that you may have eaten in Western restaurants is unlikely to be recognised as soup, let alone *borsch*, in Moscow. The best *borsch* is more like a minestrone: it is made of strong beef stock flavoured with onion and garlic in which is simmered cabbage, carrot, parsnip and beetroot, all cut into strips. Potatoes, similarly shaped, are added fifteen minutes from serving time . . . and there is, of course, sour cream in dollops riding the soup-waves of each plate. Extra colour and richness are provided by the addition of tomato purée.

Kulibiaki is perhaps their most famous fish creation. Savoury short or half puff pastry is rolled out and covered with fresh boiled salmon, also dill and sour cream, then folded up, baked and cut into slices. I have eaten some memorable fish dishes, including one that was better, easier and cheaper than our Arbroath Smokies.

You sprinkle a well-buttered oven dish with soft breadcrumbs, add strips of lightly-salted fillets of fish, like dabs or pike and dot these with more butter. Cook in a medium oven for about 15 minutes and then anoint with a custard made of three eggs beaten with half a pint of milk with pepper and dill, and bake until there is a golden crust. This dish can also be prepared in individual moulds.

Meat loaves are good, traditional, substantial Russian winter fare. Double mince the beef, add grated onions and strips of bread soaked in water; season and roll out on a floured surface. Fill the centre with boiled buckwheat or barley, fold over to make a roll and paint the outside with beaten egg and strew with breadcrumbs. Bake in a slow oven and serve with a sauce made from the juices of the pan, thickened with flour and enriched with sour cream. With this you serve mashed potatoes.

Stews (*ragus*) are common and popular. Again, sour cream, is the great leveller, whether the stew is of tongue, hare or beef.

Piroshki means 'little pie' and the diminutive is used as an endearment as well as describing the size . . . rather as East Anglians call people 'nice little old boys' even when they are 25 years old and six foot four in their socks.

Among the best was a short pastry pie filled with green onion and hard-boiled eggs, like a latter-day quiche lorraine. Deep-fried yeast pastry, filled with cabbage and hard-boiled egg also has its attraction. Make the dough, flatten it with your hand, add the filling and fold it up; allow it to rise in a warm place and fry in hot oil.

Russians have a great love of sweets which are served with tea or coffee after the meal. If you wish to end your meal in Russian style, a semolina mould with a compôte of red and black currants, damson plums and raspberries (taken from the Estonians who took it from the Danes) makes a marvellously solid ending to a solid meal.

I would also recommend *mazurka*, which is like our best Christmas cake but made with rather less flour, great quantities of dried and crystallised fruit and honey for sweetening. It sits upon the coffee table like a great, contented mahogany door-stop, moist and unrisen, to provide an all-absorbent lining for the drinks, *zanuskis* and meals that so inevitably follow.

CHINA
They are funny about times. . . .

You go to this Chinese banquet and you get pieces of dried meat and fish in a lovely sauce; then soup with eggdrop and won tun and then a steamed fish with almost raw vegetables and Peking Duck and then a bowl with noodles and lobster and dumplings and fried pieces of sweetmeat in a caramel sauce and tea . . . and you sit back wondering what else and suddenly your host says 'Hnnnk'.

You look expectantly at the interpreter and she says nothing at all. 'HHnnnnk' repeats your host and then gives a well-bred burp. After that he clears his throat and says something and smiles.

'The Minister,' says the interpreter, 'knows that you have a very busy schedule tomorrow and does not wish to detain you late into the night.'

I thank him; explain that actually my schedule is rather light and point out that it *is* only 7.45 p.m.

They bow; you bow. That's it. The evening is over; and you

wander back to the lounge of the Peking Hotel where the beneficiaries of other banquets are doing the slow fandango from the bar to the isolated easy chair that might be untenanted.

East is East wrote old Rudyard K., adding as an imbecilic addendum that West was also West and discounting their togetherness. Well, the two *do* meet, more and more often, and having spent an amazing, uplifting, instructive, obstructive (but never ever destructive), maddening, entertaining week in the capital, I am not so much an authority as a potential addict. About Chinese gastronomy, then:

You have to accept it for what it is, unlike say the Costa Blanca where, if you shout haddock and chips loudly enough, often enough, you will not only obtain it: in the fullness of time they will also bring you malt vinegar and salt in a chipped plastic container. Not so in the People's Republic.

Chinese hotel food is inexpensive, uncompulsive and quite beautifully and lovingly served. Soup comes first, reminiscent of nothing so much as that old *New Yorker* cartoon in which the waiter tells the customer, 'Chef says you're right. It was dishwater and he's sorry.' Then a tough meat and a bowl of noodles and handsomely cooked rice and the staple cabbage, boiled and oiled and baked and served. Fruit is good and plentiful and as there is no unemployment among the 900 million inhabitants, one simple hotel meal adds towards the full employment situation by necessitating a lengthy session of signing: one chit of paper for the meal, another for the beer, a third to exonerate all peoples from blame because you had no tea . . . and so on. (For the record there is no restaurant: just a series of dining rooms and the one to which you are allocated is yours for the duration of your stay.)

In countries around the world, Chinese restaurants churn out crisply pancakes and sweet and sour pork; chow mien and chop suey and meat balls. This is clearly the export side of the market . . . for those foods are as representative of the country as are whelks and cockles typical of British fare.

Peking Duck is the delicacy . . . and if the pure compulsion of a Peking Duck escapes you, I should like to declare an empathy:

I don't care for it either.

The duck is fat and is watered and dried and roasted and hung up . . . and in the end you have a magnificent mahogany-coloured skin stretched over a fatty carcase.

But a duck cooked in the manner of the people of Szechwan is a horse of an entirely different colour. You begin with a leaner bird, say a 5-pounder, and you marinate him overnight in oil and beer and herbs and spices. You then roast him for two hours in a medium oven (Gas mark 4, 350° Fahrenheit), whereafter you baste him and leave him to dry on a rack.

And then you fry the whole duck in good sesame or sunflower oil . . . though if you are a single parent family and the children have gone to bed, or if your fat pan is small, you may cut the duck into pieces and fry these individually.

The duck is served with a flourish . . . and the accompaniments are: very thin savoury pancakes (one egg, plain flour, mixture of half milk, half water, salt); spring onions cut lengthwise in one-and-a-half-inch strips, cucumber, similarly cut, and Hoi-sin sauce which is brown and unctuous and strong and available, tinned, in most oriental supermarkets. You may add spices of your own choice . . . or garlic . . . to give the Hoi-sin your own personal flavour.

The form is to spread your pancake with Hoi-sin, add scraps of well-cooked duck and crispy skin which you tear from the carcase with the traditional chop sticks (or forks), garnish with cucumber and onion, roll up and eat. The problem of what alcoholic beverage to take with a Chinese meal has not as yet been solved. In China there is wine which is white and not terribly strong nor nice. There is a Chinese spirit which is white and not terribly nice but strong . . . and there is a national beer which is probably as suitable as anything—strong, dry, Pils-like lager.

Should you find the acquisition of an entry visa to China too time-consuming, then you might do very much worse than turn your back on to the front entrance of the Victoria and Albert Museum in London and proceed down the steps of No. 10 Exhibition Road where you will find a basement restaurant called the Paper Tiger which excels in the gastronomy of the East.

As a recognised mark of approval, I have even seen in that establishment some real Chinese people; they stayed to enjoy their banquet until midnight and looked contented and at ease, although bemused by the funny shape of our eyes.

JAPAN

The consumption of Japanese food requires an enquiring mind, a strong stomach and thigh muscles of the very highest order ... and, if I advise my readers to hurry to avail themselves of the fare of which I write, it is because currently the most successful eating house in Tokyo is McDonald's; the most popular single dish a cheeseburger.

The American occupation left its mark upon the land of the rising yen with soda fountains, burger kings, ice-cream parlours and bar upon bar upon bar ... but look a little deeper (or in Tokyo a little higher, for it is not unusual to find a restaurant on the seventh floor of an office building or above a bank) and you will discover traditional Japanese restaurants aplenty.

When I left for the Far East, I had a Foreign Office briefing, in the course of which I asked whether I should take a dinner jacket. The answer was in the negative, but my mentor advised me to take a lot of good socks, and shoes that slip on and off.

His advice was sound, for the first thing you do in a Japanese eating house—or Japanese home—is to remove your shoes. Depending on the quality of the place, you then put on their 'house' shoes, or sit in your socks.

For the meal itself, you are placed on the floor—well, a cushioned part of the floor—and you tuck your feet under a table which is fifteen inches from the ground. I, personally, found this an absolutely unacceptable position in which to consume food, but I don't suppose a hundred million Japanese can be wrong ... though it is noticeable that few of them are fat.

You start with tea. Not nice Indian tea, with milk and two lumps, but green tea: tepid and brackish, opaque and emerald-coloured, like the liquid you might encounter in a frog pond towards the end of a hot summer.

As the Japanese are kind and considerate, and above all *concerned* hosts, they watch over you as you drink it.

Course follows upon course and it is not, as in Western restaurants, sort of pushed in your direction. In Japan you have at most one waitress for four customers, as often as not one each and they serve and chat and sing and pour your drink—and local etiquette demands that when you lift up the saki bowl, the waitress or geisha pours. Moreover, our custom sort of decrees that when you are holding up a filled receptacle you drink from it . . . after which geisha teaching requires that she replenish your bowl (at least you do yourself no serious injury if you fall on to the floor).

There are also interesting soups, and something called *tofu*—made of soya bean curd and looking like junket (hey: what happened to junket?)—which is diced and floats in the soups.

Fish comes next, raw or spiced—always grilled if it is cooked.

Among meat, steak is the most common—either Teriyaki which is very thinly sliced, just cooked and served with a soya sauce, Sukiyaki which is prepared for you by an attentive geisha which causes you to fail to notice how the thin strips of beef and the raw egg and the broth and the peppers and the noodles all come together.

Perhaps for the Westerner who is apprehensive of the eating habits of the East, Tempura might be the most instantly acceptable traditional Japanese confection. It is a sophisticated version of fish and chips, the Tempura chef sitting before a cauldron of very hot oil and mountains of prawns and ochra and mushrooms and courgettes and I know not what else. You order—and he picks up what you have selected in his chopsticks, gives it a fast twirl in batter and fries it to crisp deliciousness even as he marks the slate on the side of your plate so that, come the time of your account, they know how many pieces of what you have consumed.

138

For relish, there is grated giant radish which is horseradish-like. At the end of the meal they do not eat cheese, though there is inevitably a soya bean substance that is savoury. The norm is fruit, fresh or handsomely fashioned into salads and compôtes.

My first Japanese breakfast was a surprise and so to be perfectly honest were my second and third. My hosts met me with a bow and a smile and: 'You have not tried the traditional Japanese breakfast?'

'Yes,' I said the second and third times.

'Ah so.'

You take off your shoes, having only just put them on, and you sit at a low table and try to tuck your legs beneath it. Coffee is what I expected. Wrong.

You get soup. It is called miso soup and is made of fermented soya beans and seaweed. Then pickles; radishes, cucumber and sweet peppers and then a bowl of nourishing rice and a raw egg and noodles in a sea of green tea (I spilt the tea).

My hosts watched me anxiously and said: 'You do not care for Japanese breakfast?'

'I do not eat breakfast,' I said with total honesty, though even more dedicated truthfulness would have made me say that if I were a breakfast-eater, then these dishes would come some way down the order on my list of choices.

What cannot be denied is that Japanese food is very lovely to look at. At cocktail parties you get delicately pink slices of marinated raw salmon and the whitest of white rice, glutinous and large of grain, wrapped into a cylinder with a band of dark seaweed. Raw vegetables are cut with precision and expertise. Raw fish is sliced with total symmetry and arranged on dishes as handsomely as one would expect in a country in which flower arrangement seems as common a pastime as is bingo in Britain.

The Western palate is unlikely to take instantly to all that is offered the visitor . . . but there is much which is quite delicious—though not to my taste as delicious as the traditional Japanese lunch I was given at their embassy in London.

Of the memorable meals I recall one sea bass in Kyoto— as good as I have ever eaten.

On the subject of memorability, I also recall a meeting with a Minister in Tokyo at which we were served not only the inevitable tea, but a sweetmeat the size of a giant gobstopper, dark grey in colour, jellyfish-like in substance with a granulated finish and, although I might have been mistaken, it seemed to breathe in and out at irregular intervals. Mesmerised, I sat and watched for the half hour of the 'discussion'.

But if I was less than totally seduced by the oriental overtures to my stomach it would be unfair not to publish their impression of me. In the issue of *Japanese VIP* magazine, which chronicled my visit to their Tokyo Club, the author ends his article:

'Mr Freud answered our questions very rapidly in a British accent. Since he was in Japan on an official visit, he was probably a little nervous, but seemed to be the perfect English gentleman with a great sense of humour and difficult to deal with.'

USA

In England we pride ourselves on our roast beef . . . as do the French on their cassoulet, the Germans on sauerkraut, the Italians on pasta—also ice-cream—the Spaniards on paella, the Indians on curry, Mexicans on beans and Australians (if what I hear is true) on kangaroo tail soup.

In the United States there just isn't a more American dish that you can eat than Hamburgers.

As returning British soldiers throw themselves on to the soil and embrace the white cliffs of Dover, so do Americans, home from foreign parts, bury themselves in a Hamburger smothered in sauce and pickle and relish and onion and encased for good measure in a steam-baked bun.

It started at the Great Louisiana Purchase Exhibition of 1903. St Louis, then, the year after the end of the Boer War —and would you believe that at one North American shindig the fried Hamburger sandwich, the hot dog and the ice cream cone all made their first appearance? Perhaps the idea was not new, but the marketing was a wow right from the start. There was this red meat which Finns and Latvians had been scraping at with blunt knives for mid-morning snacks since pre-Napoleonic times and suddenly the Americans go and broil it and pop it into a bun and name it after a north German sea-port, and then they do roughly the same with a sausage and a bun and name it after a Prussian city.

I accept that Hamburger and Frankfurter roll off the tongue more melodiously than, say, Exeterer or Market Harborougher ... but that a way of life should be created around as plain a product; that some of the great fortunes of the Western world should have been made by mincing and cooking and then disguising the taste and hiding the stuff in a bun does make us less successful inventors feel pretty green. (I personally had great hopes for barbecued ducks' feet, served in hollowed tomatoes. To date the take-up has been very disappointing.)

But while I sit and wait for my own creations to meet with acclaim it must be reported that the Hamburger had its problems before universal acceptance and the great break-through came with what we call Take Away, the Americans call To Go and the French don't have a name for because it is not considered nice to eat in the street ... let alone in your car.

'Take Away' is now the great go-go industry in catering and Hamburgers are the diamonds in the industry's jewelbox.

Contemporary kitchens in the United States are designed to cope with this phenomenon ... many families having sold their cookers to make room for bigger trash-cans to take the wrappings and more commodious cupboard space for ketchups and relishes.

But, as much as some franchisers would have you believe that Hamburgers mature inside greaseproof wrappings, they *can* be excellent. I believe that it is the atavistic feeling of what is American is good; therefore what is unAmerican must be bad ... which has been instrumental in making people serve up Hamburgers in the amazing number of varieties currently on the market.

There is Hefty Hamburger Soup—enough for fifty, states my recipe book published in Lincoln, Nebraska ... and while I would have thought half a pint would be enough for a hundred they actually start with 7 quarts of water. But there are also Hamburgers with the subtlest of French sauces; with oriental toppings; and a Hamburger Soufflé, no less.

If you are unacquainted with the Americans' national food ... and especially if you are acquainted with it ... here, for my money, are some solid thoughts on the subject and a recipe for the very best Hamburger.

It is a mistake to think that if beef is minced it need not be high-quality meat. The better the meat the better the Hamburger ... though too many people confuse tenderness with quality. It is wasteful to make a Hamburger with fillet steak. Exceedingly sensible to use rump. Not a bad idea to use a mixture of rump and topside. If you want good Hamburger mixture do not think that what the butcher has already minced is going to be the answer to your problem. It is preferable to buy the meat and watch him mince it ... and if the mincer is in the back of the store, go elsewhere or mince your own meat when you get home.

Hamburger mixture should contain not more than 10 per cent fat. The more often you mince it (US recipes often call for double-minced beef) the more compact and heavy the Hamburger becomes.

The more you handle the mixture, the less juicy it tends to get. It is better to serve two or three smallish Hamburgers— about six ounces—than one huge one.

For my money the best Hamburger is made as follows: 1 lb rump steak, minced; 1 lb topside, minced twice; 3 tablespoons plain yogurt; 2 beaten eggs; 1 teaspoon (rounded) Dijon mustard; salt to taste; 1 level coffeespoon ground white peppercorns.

Mix the ingredients with a wooden spoon and let the mixture rest for at least an hour.

Shape into six-ounce patties. Cook on a lightly-greased surface under the fiercest pre-warmed grill for two or more minutes on each side. Do not squeeze the Hamburgers while they are being cooked.

Serve, if you must, with tomato ketchup, relish, mustard

and, if there is nothing for it, inside a bun glistening with sesame seeds.

If you are your own master—or if no one is looking—place the Hamburger on a fine porcelain plate (Royal Doulton is useful) and serve it with a salad of lettuce and green walnuts in an olive oil, lemon and sea salt dressing. A bottle of Volnay 1969 would be pleasant as an accompaniment.

MEXICO

If you were to call in Sherlock Holmes and confront him with a severed hand, grime-covered but for a small clean patch an inch wristward of the base of the thumb . . . it would be a very run-of-the-mill mystery for the great detective.

'It is the hand of a professional tequila drinker,' he would tell the oafish Watson, and warming to his theme he might explain that tequila is the juice of the spiky pineapple-like cactus-shaped maguey plant that proliferates in the foothills of the Sierra Madre around Guadalajara (the 'j' is pronounced as an 'h') in Mexico . . . (where the 'x' is also pronounced as an 'h'). He would add that the consumption of tequila is preceded by a lick of salt from the back of the hand.

I first came across the drink during England's abortive attempt to retain the World Cup in 1970 . . . and when we had lost the trophy, our honour and the best parts of our innards as a result of an affliction known as Montezuma's revenge (pronounced as it is spelt) tequila was about the only thing that made sense.

A whisky imbiber requested to induct a prospective tippler would stress the need to open the bottle; might suggest water or soda as an accompaniment and would be hard pressed to say more.

Not so the tequila pro, for the drink is the middle stage of a three-part ritual which begins with salt and ends with a wedge of lime. The technique is acquired, which the taste is not.

Stretch your hand away from you with the fingers and thumb straining towards the top of the far wall . . . or the horizon if you are currently homeless.

143

Next try to move the stiffly out-stretched thumb backwards towards the little finger and you will notice a small indentation at the very base of the thumb, which is the Mexicans' portable salt cellar.

(Some Englishmen take snuff from the very same part of the anatomy . . . so that if you produced a severed hand, clean but for a brown stain an inch wristward from the base of the thumb Sherlock Holmes would be equally quick off the mark.)

Tequila, then, is made from the fruit of the mezcal, which is grown for upwards of ten years before it is picked and hacked and cooked and distilled and then distilled again. As you pull your sombrero more comprehensively over your face in a tequilic haze, you might reflect that the plant is dead. It yields but once and once only, but weep not too copiously, for the small state of Jalisco currently grows twice as many pinos as Britain has citizens and each (pino) weighs about one hundredweight.

To put it another way the supply is good for a few months yet.

The best tequilas are as strong as the best malt whisky, some are matured in oak and acquire a golden hue and strangely these are prized hardly at all in South America. The demand is for the clear white spirit with the unique perfume of cactus and shrub of the plains of Guadelajara . . . 5,000 feet above sea level.

What is more, the best tequilas are made by the best people; unlike the manufacturers of vodka, schnapps, aquavit etc., tequila distillers are as socially desirable as are the champagne barons of France or the British beerage itself.

Basic tequila then is a quick lick of salt—and not our iodised flick - it - over - your - shoulder - when - you - spill - the - sago - pudding stuff but sharp crystals of rock or sea salt which is twice as salty—followed by a long swig of the spirit followed by a sharp squirt of lime. You allow a moment or two for reflection, before repeating the exercise.

The night after England lost to West Germany in Léon a journalist friend and I sat reflectively, each over a bottle of 96 degree proof liquor and invented what may be the first if not the only tequila game:

Two men sit in a room each with a bottle (and salt and lime); when each has emptied his bottle (also the salt and the lime) one goes out, knocks on the door and the other has to guess who it is.

I remember playing it twice that night, without actually recalling which of us won.

Now that tequila is more generally available outside Mexico (the United States currently import an annual five million gallons) the lick and gulp and squirt tequila drinkers have given way to the inventions of white-jacketed cocktail barmen.

Fortunately they can do with the stuff almost what they please, and the taste shines through.

A Margarita (called after the patron saint of social security or possibly stuffed olives), is made by rubbing the rim of a glass with lemon; dunking the rim in rocksalt which then adheres to it . . . and filling the glass with one part curacao to three parts tequila to a squeeze of lime . . . and quite a lot of chipped ice. You miss a bit of the atavistic feeling but it is a fair drink.

Other tipples are tequila sunrise: a double measure of tequila, a teaspoon syrup of grenadine, mix in a tall glass with ice and fill up with fresh orange juice.

Tequila sunset: this is a cocktail produced in a blender or liquidiser—or a small bucket powered by a strong man with a sharp fork. Three parts tequila to one part each grenadine and orange juice are blended with a few ice cubes, poured into chilled glasses and garnished with slices of fresh lime.

There is also a bloody Maria, which is a bloody Mary in which you substitute Tequila for Vodka.

A tequila sour, which is like a whisky sour . . . you've guessed it.

A Lolita, which is made by blending tequila with honey and lime juice and adding a dash of bitters to the frosted glass into which you decant this.

I can still remember the days when voyagers brought back women or unicorns from their travels; as it is now generally accepted that bottles of duty free booze are appropriate gifts, tequila just might be the answer.

CHAPTER NINE

All the year round

I have never been one for talking about the weather: that and assessing other people's photographs are subjects on which I give way to all comers, but I welcome most warmly the coming of spring.

I mean the season, not the weather. Last year it snowed in early May and my enthusiasm was not a jot less effusive. 'It is spring,' I said. 'Artichokes are in the shops and if they don't come from France, they soon will. The University cricket teams are being demolished by the Counties, if only in the bar (until they can take the covers off) and up-to-date information on the Derby is finally available: last year it was Shergar: this year the aptly named Peacetime.'

Annually, my car goes better soon after I have paid the April rates bill, and in the country hitch-hikers look more appetising, traffic policemen less menacing, phone boxes not as vandalised. It is without doubt the time to clean out the boot, dust the car rugs and give the cylinder head an extra wipe in case there really is nowhere else to fry an egg when you next want a motorised meal.

It is what Neville Cardus called 'the sweet o' the year',

which I used to think was Baked Alaska, but has something to do with putting blanco on the straps of pads.

Spring is bad news for fish and chips, a good time to take the deep-fat pan away to be re-tinned, the end of the road for nourishing soups and fatty stews because grease and spring are poor bed-fellows. Rather as any sane party-goer slurps very cold neat vodka as an interlude between the end of social cocktails and the start of serious imbibing, so might the dedicated gourmet now think about some well-constructed meal that will herald the beginning of food as opposed to the continuation of concoctions.

Food that goes with sunshine demands a new attitude: no longer are things cooked with a view to re-heating and serving as hot-pot. Food for the months without an 'r' demands an exactness of approach which is superfluous when there are fall-back dishes that can be made from what is left over.

October's boiled chicken can be minced and curried and casseroled and blanquetted. May chicken must be cooked in perfect broth until the meat is just done, ready to be jointed and slid under a coating of well-made fennel mayonnaise, or garnished with a chaudfroid sauce, which is a mixture of best thick white béchamel, double cream and enough gelatin to make the covering shine when hot, set in glazed contentedness when cool. The stock in which the fowl was cooked is reduced to form the basis of the sauce.

As the cuckoo signals the start of some environmental phenomenon, so does the first plate of vichyssoise give notice of the summer months to come. A marvellous confection, vichyssoise is ideally made with new potatoes, leeks and onions, all chopped and simmered in butter, softened in white stock and then liquidised and added to boiling cream, sieved, cooled and served with fresh chopped chives and rock salt, on plates that have been kept in the freezer.

Any tin of vichyssoise put into a liquidiser with half its volume in cream and six ice cubes seems to me to be an excellent substitute for the labour-intensive, home-made production. What matters is the creaminess, the coldness, the

147

freshness of the chives and the grit of the salt crystals as they go for the fillings in your teeth. If you must have home-made accompaniments, buy some cheese straws and sprinkle them with grated Cheddar and cayenne pepper before giving them four minutes at the top of a medium oven. 'Careful,' you say as you bring them in. 'They're very hot—just out of the oven.'

People think of sausages as a winter filler; they are wrong. Buy a pound of good pork sausages and remove the meat from the casings. You could also buy sausage-meat in a pound packet but this is harder to find.

As no sausage-meat on general sale is of the very best Harrods-Fortnum-Paxton-and-Whitfield-quality, take steps to make it so. To a pound of sausage-meat, add a pinch of mace (they never put in enough), 8 freshly crushed white pepper-corns (they use flavoured sawdust), a flat tablespoon of finely sliced onion (what they put in was dried) and four rashers of lean streaky bacon: this increases the meat content.

If you like garlic in your sausage, marinate some strips of bacon in cooking brandy and garlic overnight; add this to the sausage-meat or roll the sausage-meat around the garlicky bacon so that each sausage has such a filling.

You cook sausages on a piece of foil rubbed with oil; cook in a medium oven at 360° F, gas mark 4½ for half an hour; if they get too brown, cover with oiled foil.

Summer pudding is something about which cookery writers should not pontificate. Traditionally it is bread and berries— nicely derinded white chopped slices of bread and properly washed red or black or blue well-ripened berries, mixed to-gether with sugar that has been melted to a syrup. Put into a dish, cover with a plate on which you stand a four-pound weight and serve with fresh cream. This is only good advice if there is no one among your friends and relations whose speciality this is. There are people who swear by bread pudding, would not dream of marrying a girl who cannot make bread pudding, bore the pants off everyone who will listen to them on the subject of bread-puddings. In truth it is no more than an excuse for eating more than six jam sandwiches at one sitting.

148

The blisters are healing; breath which came, when it came, in ever shorter pants is now back to its rheumy norm. The Marathon is over; only the medals and the stories of who did what, where, with whom, remain.

On Saturday I ate pasta; the training officer for the Marathon said pasta was the very best kind of carbohydrate, carbohydrates being the very best way of building the human frame to peak fitness. Also he got 15 per cent commission from the Spaghetti House on all sales to people wearing running shoes. (He had 30 per cent commission on the running shoes.)

If you eat pasta for its carbohydrate content, buy it in tins or old packets; it is a mistake to enjoy eating what is good for you. Londoners who like pasta, should go down Old Compton Street and buy freshly made tagliatelli or lasagne which taste marvellously good and therefore less beneficial.

The starting cannon resounded at 9.30 a.m. and as even the super-optimists assessed the point of departure for non-expert runners as seven minutes later, there was time for kidneys on toast; very sustaining kidneys are—and good for you because of all the carbohydrates in the toast; just what last night's pasta needed to go on doing its job. Use Mother's Pride, thick-cut, plastic-wrapped, date-stamped, rindless, given 25 seconds each side under a grill which has been allowed to get very hot.

Split a pair of lamb's kidneys, soak overnight in milk, dry, dust in plain flour seasoned with salt and cayenne pepper, and sizzle in good dripping until the juices cease to run red and run pink. Arrange these on the toast, which you have buttered lightly. Fat is not terribly good for long-distance runners.

10 a.m., with the TV cameras zooming around and the kidneys nicely settled, it was time for the first drink. At Wapping they give free champagne to any runner who stops by the wine bar there; Wapping is some nine miles from the start and champagne is notoriously hard to drink on the run. I put into the blender four ice cubes, a small glass of Green Banana liqueur, a double vodka and a quarter of a pint of milk; whizz for 15 seconds, strain into a glass and the thick rich tipple can be slurped at very high speeds.

There were now people running on all sides, jogging, singing, panting, some gasping, a few limping. It was going to be a hot day, temperatures up in the sixties, which may not sound much to you on the dial of your central heating gauge but is plenty hot enough for a Marathon. The heat causes much of you to escape via the pores, which has got to be replaced: Frosties are good, crisped in the oven and served cool with chilled milk and Acacia honey. Very good for running is honey, due to one thing and another which is too technical to mention in a short non-medical report like this.

An ex-Arsenal footballer ran alongside the phalanx of runners, picking out celebrities: 'How are you coping?'

They seemed to be coping pretty well. 'Trif,' they said, which is shorthand for tremendous, or some word like that.

After an hour the leaders had covered a dozen miles and were racing past whelk stalls. I had some smoked salmon, thickly cut on very fresh brown bread generously spread with Marks and Spencer butter spiked with pepper and lemon juice. Funny thing about fish barrows in the East End of London. Not far from many popular pubs you find the homes of SDP leaders or whelk stalls; at the latter you can get eels and cockles and mussels etc.; also wadges of not very fresh white bread and bottles of chilli vinegar.

The British catering trade is nicely geared to British independence—not for us the unctuous servility of the Europeans —but when it comes to whelk stalls I wonder whether we do not take the independence a shade too far. Deaf, belligerent bruisers stand behind the fish and it is you who beg and scrape and ask whether it is too much trouble to have a plastic fork; if the fish is less than fresh, you would be very ill-advised to mention it.

The red-headed winner raced on to Westminster Bridge; I had decided to pace myself, taking some refreshment every twenty minutes or so and it was time for something a little more substantial than the nicely calculated snippets of less or more.

Coffee and Waffles. Blue Mountain coffee ground in a small grinder which I use for peppercorns; this imparts an acceptable sharpness, and the coffee residue in the pepper is no bad thing either. Waffles are delicious; I came across them again the other day in the Waffle Shop in Norwich where you can get the most delicately crisp, hot, fresh, golden waffle for 35p, with butter *in situ* and maple syrup on the tables—where lesser places have ketchup. On Marathon Day I had mine with slices of crisply fried streaky bacon, with the rind off so that I would not be reminded of British Rail.

'Boots, boots, boots, boots,' wrote Kipling at the turn of the century; here it was shoes, shoes, and more shoes. One pair contained a woman from Watford who looked as if she had not had a square meal for weeks.

I had a brandy and ginger ale with ice cubes and a curlicue of lemon rind because it was Sunday. The lady finished in under two and a half hours which must have pleased people in Watford; if she plays her cards right, Elton John might buy her.

Now people were finishing in droves, when previously they broke the tape in trickles.

All that pasta had nearly done its job, and I sipped my second brandy and decided that a nice dish of turnip *au gratin* would see me through the next half hour. Turnips never sound as nice as do *navets* which is their French equivalent; they are delicious nevertheless.

For one athlete—in his fourth hour at the Marathon—buy a pound of baby turnips, peel them and cut them into quarters. Put them into a pan with cold salted water, engage over a low flame and when the water boils, remove pan from stove. Take half a pint of the turnip water, add half that quantity in double cream and one ounce of butter rubbed into one ounce of flour. Whisk this as it comes to the boil over a slow flame, add turnips, boil for two minutes, no more, and garnish with cubes of white bread which you bake on a buttered tray in a hot oven under a sprinkling of grated cheese.

A pint of Pimm's No. 1 made with Seven-Up and a dash of apricot brandy came next—just to replace some of the liquid I had lost trying to keep up with the other athletes.

Next year I hope they show the whole race on one channel.

Food writers dread the summer.

In early spring they waffle about the first leek and the last oyster. Asparagus is next, then gulls' eggs, strawberries, salmon trout ... and after that mid-August heralds the grouse, September the blackberry, October the pheasant followed by the long build-up to Christmas and the short count-down from Seville oranges. But come the summer, the world demands a piece on beach food; what to take for a day by the sea that is not bloater paste sandwiches.

I should like to place on record that the one thing which is absolutely essential, if you are going to indulge in what the French call '*le pique-nique sur la plage*' is a refrigerator. You can now buy refrigerators that run off car batteries—if you can get the car on the beach—but if you can get a car on the beach you can drive it to the nearest hostelry. If I had shares in the car battery fridge company I should sell before they rumbled us.

Environmentalists, who get several per cent of the County Council vote in Cornwall, go on and on about solar energy. What amazes me is why, when there is the occasional burst of solar about, no one has invented a solar-powered ice-box. I would buy shares in that company and hold on to them.

Let me tell you about food on a beach. You only need it, only feel like eating it, when the sun is not shining and then you might as well slope off the beach and find a pub. When the sun blazes down on the Ambre Solaire where your hair used to be, there is little attraction in tepid chicken and limp salad. Who wants a Thermos flask of white coffee? How do you keep sand out of bananas? What price a bag of crisps flavoured with essence of buzzard?

You need a drink and the drink needs a refrigerator. It is as simple as that. There is a lukewarm argument in favour of tying a piece of string around the neck of a champagne bottle and floating it out into the cool sea; it does not work. If the day is hot enough, the sea is warm enough—which is not cold enough for white wine. You need a refrigerator.

A District Council black plastic bag filled with ice is an idea but it is very heavy and unwieldy. The ice has to be chopped up to surround and thereby cool the bottles and chopped ice melts very quickly. By the time you have carted it across the sands and checked to see that the contents are still cold, you don't have a lot of wine left. I speak from experience.

If they can provide life-guards and life-buoys and life-boats and life-belts, why cannot they have jump-leads and light-weight ice-boxes that you can plug in and produce ice in the time in which you can boil water by means of other appliances? After all, the average British beach temperature is very much closer to freezing than boiling, so it should be easier, not harder. They make portable radios and portable televisions which are useless on beaches. What research is being done on portable refrigerators? Man has reached the moon; why can't a fridge get on to a beach?

About ten years ago, I sailed from Cape Town to Rio de Janeiro—which looks marvellously far if you have a map of the world on which one city is to the extreme left, the other on the far right. We had no refrigeration and I constructed an ice-box that kept food and drink cold for a fortnight. I took a huge wooden crate, insulated it with oiled silk and lined the bottom with dry ice wrapped in newspaper; put in alternate layers of food and wrapped dry ice, and covered the box with a tarpaulin. It worked because the box was in the coolest part of the ship; it is different on a beach where there are no cool parts. You need a refrigerator because you need drink and on a hot day drink must be cold.

Failing drink at the right temperature, you might as well cook something hot and nourishing, if only to keep your mind off a Godfather—which is a measure of Amaretto to three measures of whisky, the glass filled with crushed ice.

On a beach in Northern Ibiza, before the bowling alley and the package tours came to the island, I once witnessed a family making a paella. They brought a frying pan twenty inches in diameter—and if you are a party of 37, which they were, you would be foolish to attempt this dish with a smaller vessel. For a party of eight you need a pan of about twelve inches diameter. You also have to build a fire, which uses up quite a lot of the day (or you can buy an outdoor cooking set and attendant charcoal).

In the way of food: two small chickens, cut into joints; one and a half pints of mussels, or half a pint if they are peeled; two dozen small scallops, cut in quarters; one pound each of rough chopped onion, red and green sweet peppers cut in strips, and tomatoes cut in chunks.

Heat half a pint of oil in the pan and fry the chicken pieces and onion; then add other ingredients. When all is nicely cooked, about ten to fifteen minutes, add three half-pint glasses filled with Patna long-grained rice and just under five half-pint glasses of water, also salt, pepper and saffron. Stir until the water simmers and then batten down the fire and let it cook very gently until the rice has drunk all the liquid and is soft.

You serve this with large glasses of Sangria made by adding one bottle of lemonade to two bottles of wine, some chopped fruit and a lot of ice. If you have enough of this, bloater paste sandwiches are a very nice accompaniment. Children can have have crisps.

It was Wordsworth who wrote:

> *Give all thou canst; high Heaven rejects the lore*
> *Of nicely-calculated less or more.*

Well, nicely-calculated less or more is exactly what entertaining people tends to be about:

'Shall we give them smoked salmon?'

'They only gave us melon.'

'But it was Ogen melon.'

'Must we open the 1971 claret for them?'

'They did have Pam and Giles to stay at their Paris flat.'

When it comes to open-air food, 'nicely-calculated less or more' hardly figures. Outside the four walls of your house, guests marvel at anything better than a fish-paste sandwich and clap their hands in delight if the Thermos contains more than coffee.

In the beginning, al fresco meals were pretty much the same as those partaken of in the dining room. Servants were despatched ahead with mahogany table, Chippendale chairs, damask cloths, fine bone china and sterling silver cutlery. The chef was already there with his field kitchen, just like the one they used for the officers in the last war . . . and in those days there was always a last war in clear memory, frequently a last-war-but-one as well.

The gentry arrived and partook of brown windsor soup, fillets of halibut, baked meats, roasted game and whatever else was the order of the season. The difference between a meal in and a meal out was that the staff had to work harder when you ate out, and if you were unlucky there were flies and mosquitos which gave you something to talk about when you next had a meal in. There followed an era when the rich had hampers and the poor wrapped up food in grease-proof paper. Those days are over, too.

Today's outdoor gastronome has a barbeque or Bar-B-Q and the interesting thing about these is that men who would not dream of going into a kitchen, let alone cook, do the whole outside bit with huge enthusiasm, often some skill, too.

Men who sniff petulantly when the little woman scorches a piece of toast, burn whole sides of pork at the bottom of the garden and tell you that it is a job well done. 'Black on the outside, pink in the middle, ho ho ho,' and they take another huge slurp of hard liquor; for some, as yet unresearched, reason, hard liquor and cooking at the bottom of the garden go hand in glass, or do I mean glove?

Shops that cater for the man who has become so important that simple presents will not do sell Bar-B-Q sets. The expensive ones have sturdy tripods upon which you engage the container holding charcoal, above which you place the grid. Brushes for oiling the grid cost extra and should be bought by anyone who did not think of oiling the meat or fish instead. Skewers with wooden handles—and tongs for turning whatever it is you cook that was not threaded on to a wooden handled skewer—are other essentials which they will give you so long as you give them money. I maintain that one can do very well without any adjuncts and shall go on maintaining this until someone persuades me otherwise or gives me a set.

There is no great expertise involved in lighting the charcoal, oiling the chop, turning it and cooking it. The two things that separate the run of the mill Bar-B-Q attendant from his cousin who is famed throughout the neighbourhood for the quality of his fare are the liquor in which the food is marinated and the sauce that is served with it when it is cooked.

Let us begin with the marinade.

When you roast, bake or braise food, its lengthy sojourn in oven, pot or pan allows it to take on board such seasonings and flavourings as you add. Not so on a Bar-B-Q where you present the item to a fierce flame for the shortest possible time consistent with being able to say, 'This has been cooked,' or, at the very least, 'This is *not* raw.'

The marinade must contain oil for lubrication, tenderising and mobility on the grill; pepper and mustard (no salt as salt in meat-marinade makes for toughness) and what you will of garlic or onion, herbs, spices and syrups.

As there are still those who like it all set down in writing (*whaddeyer mean erbspicesnsyrups?*), here is what you might do if you have a dozen people and intend to give each of them sausages, chops and chicken legs.

To make basic marinade: ¾ pint corn oil; 1 dessertspoon Worcester sauce; 24 crushed peppercorns (about a teaspoon); 2 shakes of Tabasco; 1 dessertspoon corn syrup.

Do not waste time marinating the sausages—just brush them with the mixture when it is time to cook them. Divide the marinade equally into two bowls: to one, add a large clove of garlic, crushed, a rounded dessertspoon of Italian herbs and a teaspoon of Dijon mustard. Put the chops into this.

Add to the other: 1 tablespoon grated onion and one of tomato paste, a teaspoon of curry-paste and another of paprika. Allocate this to the chickens.

The best way of marinating economically is to use plastic bags into which you put meat and liquor, expel air, tie up and turn now and then. Meat should be kept in marinade for up to 24 hours, but if time is short, heat the marinade and it will do its job in a couple of hours or even less.

We now come to the Bar-B-Q sauce: let me begin by saying

that one sauce is not enough, not if you want to make your name as an exponent of this art-form. You can buy sauces and decant them into bowls to make it look as if it was all your own work. If deceit has no appeal, a sweet spiced sauce is best made by chopping 4 ounces of candied fruit, adding 4 tablespoons redcurrant jelly melted in a pan (must not boil) with a similar quantity of port or sweet sherry and incorporating two tablespoons of hot Dijon mustard or $1\frac{1}{2}$ of English mustard which is hotter.

A green sauce is produced by adding a rounded tablespoon each of chopped parsley, chopped watercress, chopped gherkins, chopped capers and finely chopped onion to a 10-ounce carton of soured cream.

Try a red sauce: 4 tablespoons of tomato paste enriched with the oil and chopped fillets of two small tins of anchovy, one tablespoon grated horseradish and two cloves of crushed garlic.

So much for cooking.

The good outdoor caterer will have an array of appetite-sating first courses to see his guests through to the high point of his performance . . . when he shouts whatever he decides to shout and dispenses the sizzling meat on to the disposable plate.

A large bowl of sliced avocado with lemon juice and sugar is excellent and appetising at any temperature. The criterion of 'good-at-any-temperature' is important and disqualifies soups, salads and puddings from discriminating picnic menus.

Rice mixed with peas and diced sweet peppers bound in mayonnaise is useful. A dish of small mushrooms cooked in white wine, drained and dressed with tomato paste, olive oil and soured cream is acceptable hot, cold and tepid . . . and tepid is the most likely outdoor temperature.

And so to the final course. If you have been sensible, this is of no importance at all. By the time the last sausage has been prised from the grill, no one should be sober enough to tell a crêpe suzette from a dishcloth . . . which reminds me: provide a lot of damp dishcloths, ideally hot ones, but tepid will do if you cannot be bothered to wrap them in foil, and keep them on the perimeter of your charcoal.

Comes the autumn and thanks to what sociologists call 'progress' nothing much changes except the colour of the leaves. We had autumn weather for most of the summer; traditional autumn fruit is now sprayed with a mixture of lard and Windolene and the thin enveloping film preserves the fruit the whole year through. Admittedly, only swine shoot partridge and pheasant in the hatching season, but if you are rich and your freezer is big enough, the other three seasons of the year hardly inconvenience the game-bird eater at all.

I know that autumn is here when the last night of the Proms causes me to prepare red, white and blue sandwiches for the musical side of the family, and when Cartmel, Kelso, Sedgefield, Bangor-on-Dee and Uttoxeter come back into business as race-tracks. On a few selected wintry days between October and April moderate racehorses jump fences and hurdles for modest prizes, watched by thoughtful, knowledgeable crowds for whom the sport is as important as the gamble.

Now in France country tracks are a gastronomes' dream; not only do the neighbouring towns and villages put their best oven forward to seduce race-goers into stopping for a fillet of pork baked into a brioche (served with ravigotte sauce), but the course authorities lease to the most prestigious charcutiers and boulangers the concessions to look after the inner man before, during and after the serious business of racing. Indeed, there are those who go to the track, eat and leave before the first contest.

At Australian country meetings I have paid £1 to take a plate and carve myself slices from a luxuriantly steaming ham, whose cousins simmered invitingly in an adjacent cauldron. The caterers did well out of this capital-intensive exercise, as did their customers.

Until Egon Ronay publishes an up-to-date gastro-guide to the race-courses of Britain, the punter at large will only suspect that old cheese sandwiches are not an essential attribute to a day at a National Hunt course. There is no required connection between the quality of the racing and that of the service provided; on the contrary, it is often easier to do well in low wage areas, for small crowds, at predictable intervals.

Of course catering for 'events' is beset with problems and our weather—which can and does cause last-minute cancellations—makes the whole venture into a gamble. My assertion is that it is a good gamble and with a surrounding community of understanding people it should not be too difficult to make contingency plans for the disposal of the more expensive items of food.

An excellent egg and watercress sandwich, with butter on thin-cut white or brown bread, costs a basic nine pence; add two or three pence for the labour cost of preparation and at 40p a round, which is the average sale price, you stand to lose 12p, or make 30p if the sun shines. The average outside caterer who serves the racing public sticks to a very limited number of poor quality butties which run out during or soon after the third race (or remain in his proud possession for the weeks to come).

Let us be constructive: there are race-courses that sell imaginative fare, like Stratford with a fish bar, and some jolly nice jellied eel men who hawk their excellent fare in the Midlands and East Anglia. They serve soup at Huntingdon, which is sometimes better than elsewhere, but there is no small course (with the exception of Wincanton where they have farmed out the bars to different local pubs) to which I would go for the non-racing aspects of the occasion.

I shall send a magnum of vintage claret to the first clerk of the course to show genuine enterprise in course catering and I doubt not that he will receive great kudos from people who matter to him more than I do.

Instead of the surly ladies who sell you a lunch ticket for £4.50—and watch you dispassionately as you await the soup, cold tongue and salad and potatoes and trifle and cheese—why not a Chinese take-away? What would be the problems of serving hot mulled wine at the bars? One National Hunt race-goer in three shoots, eats or cooks pheasant; I have yet to see a course where they serve pheasant pie.

A barbecue is warming, attractive, quick and the fare that comes from its embers can be delicious: barbecued sausages, cutlets, hamburgers, chicken quarters would all sell and, in the event of cancellation, would all be taken at a small discount by the surrounding supporters of a caring course-community.

There are doughnut machines on the market that turn out four hundred golden jam-filled pieces an hour. I have seen them at country fairs, never on a country race-track.

For sheer quality one goes to the car park and rumbles around in the baskets which lodge in the boots of friends' cars— and the friends only bring their own food because they have despaired of finding edible fare for sale. Very few people bring their own for economic reasons.

English farmhouse cheeses are exhibited at beer festivals, not on race-courses. I have seen marvellous shows of ham for the delectation of a few hundred hungry people. A buffet of York and Suffolk and Wiltshire and Black Bradenham, with fresh wholemeal bread and butter in tubs, would make me willingly travel an extra fifty miles to watch my sport. It would also be a splendid promotion, aimed at making people eat ham again; the manufacturers might even be persuaded to sponsor a race, or buy Aintree. The whole industry seems to me to be wide open to revitalisation.

When I began to be a journalist, some 25 years ago, I wrote of football in the *Observer*. People used to ring up on Sundays and say, 'I liked the way you wrote, "Smith passed the ball to Jones who flicked it to Mackenzie's forehead from which it sped into the back of the net." Nice bit of prose, that.'

That was just about the most rewarding part of being a journalist. I widened my scope from football to cricket to boxing to Olympics; I moved from one paper to another to another, took in cooking and politics, wrote features and leaders, and the more I wrote, the better I got, the more I was paid and the less people telephoned. When they did, it was to complain: 'not as good as usual' from friends and an occasional 'a bit disappointing, that last one' from editors.

In November, a firm called Corning gave me an award of two tickets to anywhere in the world, plus hotel and restaurant charges, for becoming one of their selected food writers of 1981.

It has made up for about twenty years of not getting phone calls from readers.

I thought you would want to know and I want Corning to know that, as Liberace used to say, 'I am reely grateful, I mean that.' Only I mean that.

We spent Thanksgiving Day in a large, plush hotel in Phoenix, Arizona. Thanksgiving Day was the occasion upon which the Pilgrim Fathers celebrated their first crop and then the next and the next. Thirty years ago it was stabilised—to be acknowledged upon the last Thursday of November—so that a long weekend could be had by one and all.

The majority of feasts owe their creation to the fact that it marked the ending of a fast. You fasted and whatever you ate after you had consumed nothing at all tasted good. In God's good time, people took pains to make it taste better, which is how the tradition of feasts came about.

The Americans have pre-Thanksgiving Sales and post-Thanksgiving Sales as well as Thanksgiving offers, Thanksgiving rebates, discounts and unique opportunities, and the nation belches benevolently and eats roast turkey and dressing (which is what they call stuffing because they don't think stuffing is a nice expression). This is followed by pumpkin pie.

When it all began, turkeys were wild, stuffing was how they used flavoured cereal to make the scraggy meat go further and, as pumpkin tastes of hardly anything at all, making it into a pie and adding sugar seemed like a good idea at the time; plastic was not discovered until 250 years later.

The plush hotel in Phoenix, Arizona, certainly entered into the spirit of Thanksgiving; as a mark of general gratitude, they began by killing oysters and mussels, crabs and lobsters, prawns and scallops, mackerel, herring, salmon, sole, trout and turbot and served it in sauces, vinaigrettes and mayonnaises. Then they pulled up asparagus and mushrooms, celery and artichokes and presented pâtés, sausages, quiches, pizzas, terrines, and smoked hams, with attendant melons, papayas, mangoes, grapefruit, bananas and uglies. Glory be to Reagan, we cried as we re-re-filled our plates from the buffet. (Champagne was available on a 'pour your own, we aren't looking' basis) and then we had hot roast beef and ham and turkey and lamb because, to give true thanks, they had killed all that flesh and fowl and got a chef to carve it into thick slices; with it there came veal and oyster dressing, baked yams, Brussels sprouts and roasted potatoes, which just about kept the wolf from the door till it was time to consume pies and puddings, cakes and fruit, tarts and charlottes, custards, caramels, mousses with cream and an amazingly alcoholic sweet mince in puff pastry.

We gave thanks to Alka Seltzer and our comfortable hotel beds and swore we would never eat anything again, not ever and that evening we dined in a restaurant called Etienne which, our limousine driver said, was 'just the place for an international gourmet like you'.

I used to complain that restaurants confused the relative attractions of quality and quantity; the nastier things were, I maintained, the more they gave you, on the basis of never mind the item, feel the size. I withdraw that opinion: when you get what we got, there descends an all-enveloping contentedness from which one's critical faculties are wholly eliminated.

Heaven help my family this Christmas, let alone this Xmas.

Oyster and veal stuffing—by virtue of the high asking price of oysters—is a dish for only the very rich in the land. But there are tinned oysters—also tinned smoked oysters, which permeate oysterishness quite disproportionately to their volume.

For very excellent oyster stuffing, take 2 small tins of smoked oysters, chopped but not too finely chopped and add with all the juices to $1\frac{1}{4}$ lb minced veal, 2 beaten eggs, 6 ounces white breadcrumbs, 1 tablespoon grated onion, a teaspoon of oregano or basil, salt and pepper. Wrap in well-buttered muslin (an old nappy will do) and roast inside the turkey. It starts to get delicious after an hour and a half's cooking and keeps its quality thereafter.

For his birthday there was probably no more than a slice of unleavened bread, a piece of dried fish and a glass of sweet wine, but all over the Christian world December 25th has become an occasion for serving the most prestigious food on the best plate.

In Central Europe it tends to be goose, as often as not baked in honey and stuffed with prunes and apples. In Scandinavia, it is the Christmas cake which commands attention, layers upon layers of almond rings, decorated with glacé fruit, paper flags and spun sugar.

In Eastern Europe the cakes are soft, spiced with ginger and allspice, cinnamon and molasses and the shapes are of Christmas trees and reindeers and Father Christmasses by the half dozen, all holding hands—provided the baker's hand was steady as he removed the confection from the oven tray. I have celebrated Christmas with reindeer and with venison (both cooked). I have had a Christmas ... well Xmas ... dinner of Queensland mud crab and I have no doubt that Chinese Christians will celebrate in their own especial way with an extra course or two on top of the six that are a part of the everyday Chinese feast.

But for British readers it is not of birds' nest soup nor stewed missionary that I write.

The menu is turkey followed by Christmas Pudding and as any cookery book will give you an indication of how to cook each of these courses, I will engage your time by telling you what my fellow scribes tend to ignore.

Turkey might be a splendid animal to keep as a pet or train to do backward somersaults ... but as a dish for the oven it has very serious drawbacks. It contains the white meat of the breast and wings ... and the brown meat of the legs; very regrettably these demand quite different methods of preparation: in a nutshell, the white meat needs to be subjected to a gentle heat over a period of time ... and as the meat is dry it requires attention and basting. The brown meat, ideally, demands a short, sharp roast to cook the meat and crisp the skin.

To my mind the most satisfactory way of combating the design of this maddening bird is to perfect the cooking of the white meat and ignore the brown which will look after itself.

Take the turkey . . . and the wider and whiter the breast, the better the bird . . . and fill the inner cavity with a couple of oranges roughly cut up . . . and a couple of onions spiked with cloves. That will give you a pleasant aroma from the inside.

Stand the turkey on a large piece of foil, truss the legs tightly into the body and prepare the following paste: 1 dessertspoon Colman's mustard powder; 1 dessertspoon Worcester sauce; 2 dessertspoons salt; 1 teaspoon freshly ground black pepper (or crush up 24 peppercorns in coffee grinder or blender); 1 rounded tablespoon black treacle.

Mix the ingredients well . . . if it is very cold in your house you may have to heat them slightly in a pan. Then paint the turkey all over with the mixture. Loosely fold the foil around the bird and bake him for 6 hours (if the turkey weighs over 14 lb, give an extra hour per 3 lb.) on gas mark $1\frac{1}{2}$ which is about 285°F. It is wise to put the foil-wrapped bird on to a deep baking tray and make a few holes into the base of the foil so that the juices can run out . . . there will be a lot of very delicious juice—which will jelly when cold.

That is the best way of cooking turkey I know . . . but for Christmas, it is not just the turkey that matters . . . it is the trimmings and this is where skill and enterprise are needed.

Bread sauce: grate one large onion and simmer it in a pint of milk to which you have added four whole cloves tied in muslin, salt and ground white pepper and two ounces of butter. After ten minutes, add six slices of thick-cut bread, rindless and chopped into very small cubes. Let this simmer for another two or three minutes, remove the cloves and decant into a dish. Top with a thin covering of double cream. A quarter of an hour before bread sauce is due, place the dish in the bottom of the oven; stir in the cream just before serving.

Sausages: get these from a health food shop . . . the more expensive the better they tend to be. Brush the sausages with butter and grill them under the coolest possible grill that will cause them to sizzle. Turn them frequently and do not pierce the skin which only lets the goodness run out and is a cowardly way of ensuring that the skin will not burst . . . which it will not under low heat and careful attention. Let the sausages keep hot in loosely-wrapped foil, anointed with a knob of butter, a teaspoon of redcurrant jelly and another of liquid English mustard, in the bottom of a low oven.

Cranberry sauce: buy this. Add a teaspoon or two of sweet sherry, mix well and serve cold.

Stuffing: do not put this inside the turkey ... a method which is invidious and only means you have to dig it out again when people might be watching. Buy 2lb good sausage meat from the butcher, season it with salt and pepper and mace and fresh sage (or dried or bottled) and add an egg yolk and a whole egg and a quarter of the weight of the sausage meat (8 oz) in puréed chestnut—which comes in tins. Also the liver of the turkey cut in very thin strips and kept overnight in a bowl with a tablespoon of brandy, a grated onion of medium size and a wineglass of stout. Mix well, put into a greased baking dish and cook slowly for the last couple of hours with the turkey.

Sprouts will have been cooked for two thirds of their required cooking time and then finished off in butter and cream in a pan with tightly-closed lid—and the potatoes will be new and garnished with chives ... you will see that the turkey (while it has pride of place) could, at a pinch, be replaced by almost any other piece of white meat.

When it comes to Xmas Pudding, the packaging of fruit is currently such that it is impossible to make a single pudding without having so many ounces each of currants, raisins, sultanas, glacé fruit, peel and nuts left over. Buy a pudding ... Marks and Spencers make the most delicious ones ... and dress it with brandy butter ... 6oz butter mixed with 2oz caster sugar into which you blend a sherry glass of brandy.

Also double cream. And don't forget to pour a little warm brandy over the pudding—prior to showing it a lighted match.

These are the hedgehog days. The flesh, at the last count, was getting weaker. As I plod further along the path on the cemetery side of 50, thoughts concern themselves with chestnut stuffing and roasted pheasants; bubble and squeak, dressed crab, lobster mousse, bread and butter pudding, devils on horseback . . . and I order a softly poached egg on brown toast.

My eyes are bigger than my stomach and were it not for the fact that I share an office with Brother Smith (C., Lib., Rochdale) I should be as seriously concerned about my stomach as he is about the size of my eyes.

It is not that I am 'off' food; I worry a lot about food, I dream of food, I order food, I buy food; I just cannot eat the stuff because I ate some half an hour ago and am bound to do so again any minute now . . . I have been topping up gently ever since Christmas.

As the kitchen is very much part of my life, and there is no cooking for the present, I look to the future. Preserve, it is called. Also 'bottle' and while we are at it, 'jug', 'barrel', 'vat'; even pickle is all right because, try as you will, there is no way that you can dispose of a gallon of pickle at elevenses.

The good news on the preserving front is that Seville oranges are in the shops and this is therefore the time of year for marmalade. The inexpensive method of producing home-brand *confiture d'orange* is to get a saucepan which is at least ten inches in diameter, six inches deep and place into it four jars of Elsenham Marmalade. Add luke-warm water to reach to the tops of the labels and put on a low gas. When the labels come off (this should not take more than a few minutes) remove the jars, wipe them with a clean cloth and replace the void on the jar with a message of your own, including the date and place.

There is an expensive way which involves going out and shopping for preserving pans and jars and lids; also sugar and pectin and sweet oranges and their Spanish cousins, not to mention lemon, grapefruit and ginger. You 'prepare' the fruit and there are some that remove the pith. Juggle to produce the correct blend of sweetness and tartness; 2 sweet, 10 Seville and 1 grapefruit, $1\frac{1}{2}$ medium sized lemons, I used to think was a good blend. Then I changed my mind about the lemons. If you count the time that you spend on making marmalade, including the time spent shopping (always count your own time at what you could have earned addressing envelopes, cleaning windows or sewing mailbags), add to it the price of the ingredients and the cost of gas or electricity, you will race to Fortnum and Mason and buy the ready-made stuff. Man, or woman for that matter, can only—should only—make so many pounds of marmalade a year; how else does one occupy the culinary winter evenings!

Colonel Kenney Herbert, who soldiered in Madras in the latter part of the last century, is a man whose writing I much admire.

On the subject of sauces, upon which he was a great expert (if you can be an expert when the top of your palate is likely to have been removed by half a century of munching Madras curries) he gave the advice, 'I denounce Worcester Sauce and Tapp's Sauce as agents far too powerful to be trusted to the hands of the native cook.' These sound like the words that could emanate from Mrs Thatcher's own little fellow in Number 10; the ingredients for Tapp's are as available now as they are in the peacock spring, and I can think of little that is more acceptable than a well-made jar of Tapp's and the smell of the production is one that the whole neighbourhood will savour with rapt enjoyment.

Here is a recipe straight from *Indian Domestic Economy*, 1850: Take of green sliced mangoes, salt, sugar and raisins each 8 ounces. Red chillies and garlic each 4 ounces, green ginger 6 ounces. Vinegar three bottles. Lime juice one pint. Pound several ingredients well (he means the ginger, chillies and garlic), add the vinegar and lime juice, stop the vessel close and expose it to the sun for whole month stirring or shaking it well daily. Then strain it through a cloth and cork tight. PS. The residue makes an excellent chutney.

Well, the thing about the 'sun for a month' is going to be tricky but a linen cupboard for four weeks could have a similar effect; further, the back page of *The Times* suggests inexpensive tours to warm places—where there is no extra charge for taking a few drums of Tapp's searching for maturity.

Great thing about sauces such as this is that they revive the appetite; this is pretty important in these rhinoceros days in which we find ourselves.

Index

Page references in *italic* indicate a useful hint or tip. Those in **bold** indicate a complete recipe, or enough information to construct a dish.

Adnams (brewers) 117
Agneau, gigot roti, 61
Ale, mild, 8
Alka Seltzer, 64, 162
All Bran, 129
Almonds:
  ground, 19
  salted, **44**
Aphrodisiacs, 5, **7**
Apple pie, *37, 66*
Apples, 72, 112:
  Cox's Orange Pippin, 72
  Kingdom, 119
Apple sauce, brandied, 94
Apricot brandy, 7, 151
Arbroath smokies, **130**
Armagnac, 62, 99
Artichokes, 15, 92, 161
Asparagus, 14, *63,* 103, 152, 161
Aspirins, 8
Avocado:
  stuffed, 71
  with lemon juice and sugar, **76**

Babycham, 110

Bacon, 114, 126, 150:
  rind, 129
Baked Alaska, 146
Baking powder, 18
Bananas, 53, 65, 152, 161:
  grown-ups' milk shake, **149,**
  milk shake, **68**
Banquets, 47:
  Chinese, 134
Barbeques, 155–7, 159:
  sauces, 157
Barley, 50, 102
Beans, 140:
  baked, 21, 67
  green, 59
  runner, 65
  shoots, 55
Beef, 140:
  consomme, 42
  pot roast, **29**
  potted, 96
  roast 162
  Scots, 130
  sliced, 72
Beer, 116–7:

Chinese, 136
festivals, 119, 160
Beurre manie, 12
Biscuits, 4:
　Bath Oliver, 42, 64
　brownies, 46
　Garibaldi, 2
　packets of, 72
　Ritz, 29, 103
　water, 64–5
Bisto, 80
Blackberries, 152
Black pudding, 46, 53
Borsh, **132–3**
Bouillon, 50
Bovril, 72
Brandy, 151:
　butter, 165
Brawn, 126
Bread, 16, **17**, 97; to keep fresh, *26*;
　to refresh, *98*, *101*:
　baking 'in the round', **20**
　brown bread, 21, 25, 65, 150
　and butter, 30, 65, 71, 113, 114, 160
　and butter pudding, 69, 166,
　crusty loaves, 22
　French, 99
　fried, **116**
　fruit loaves, 18, 25
　garlic bread, 21
　Hovis, 2, 99, 103,
　Mother's Pride, 110, 111, 149
　rolls, 18, 30
　sauce, **164**
　Scotch baps, 72, 99, 119
　sticks, 18, 30
Breakfast, 19, 62, 114–6, 125, 130:
　Japanese, 139
Brioche, 114:
　with pork, 158
British Rail, 71–3
Broth, 43, 50, **51-2**:
　sheep's head, 47
Brussels sprouts, 129, 162, **165**
Bubble and squeak, 165
Burgundy, 1, 127
Butter, 11, 22, 25, 26, 34, 72, 101,
　150:
　flavoured butter, 30
　sauce, 14
　unsalted, 62, 116

see also Bread

Cabbage, 131
Cakes, 24, 73, 162:
　Christmas, 163
　Marks and Spencer's, 163
　Mr Kipling's, 73
Calf's head, 110
Calf's liver hot pot, **88**
Calvados, 66
Canapés, 103
Candles, birthday, 20
Cape gooseberries, 62
Carbonnade, 56
Carrots, 11, 59, 69, 108
Cassis, 63
Cassoulet, *12*, 140
Caterers *see* Restaurants and caterers
Caviare, 131, 132:
　Beluga, **62**
　Poor Man's, **132**
　Sevruga, 120
Celeriac, 108
Celery, 30, 88–90, 161:
　hotpot, **88**
　soup, **88**
　trifle, 89
Champagne, 9, 27, 62, 63, 104, 149,
　152, 161:
　for breakfast, 115
　for tea, 120–1
　with scrambled eggs, 126
Chanterelles, **64**
Cheese, 37, 69, 98, 131; for breakfast,
　114:
　blue Cheshire, 64
　Brie, 108
　burger, 43, 55, 137
　cake, 53
　Cheddar etc, 27, 72
　cream, 24, **54**
　farmhouse, 27, 72, 119, 160
　Marks and Spencer's, 36
　stale, *39*
　Stilton, 42, 108, 122
　straws, 2, 48, *148*
Chelsea Bun, 71
Chicken, *3*, 97, 129:
　à la Freud, **61**
　boiled, 65, 80, 147:
　boiled in cider, **79**

cold, 72
ginger, 80
legs, 111
legs, to barbecue, 156
lemon, **75**
liver terrine, 99–100
Marks and Spencer's, roast, 36
Maryland, *60*
restaurant descriptions of, 58
roast, to reheat, *97*
steamed, 10
tarragon, **80**
Children, 12, 37, 110
Chili con carne, 58
Chili peppers, 47
Chinese food, 134–6:
  takeaway, 11, 159
Chips, 7, 44, 103, 111
Chocolate, 33:
  bitter with crystallised ginger, 49
  drinking, 34
  flake, 48
Chopping and slicing, *5*
Chops, 156
Chop suey, 135
Chow mien, 135
Christmas cake, 163
Christmas pudding, 129, 163, 165
Chutney, 44, 72, 99, *100*, **167**:
  green tomato, 126
  Marks and Spencer's apricot, 36
Cinnamon, 115, *124*:
  toast, 120–1
Citron pressé, **75**
Claret, 1, 36, 42, 43, 70, 154, 159
Clootie dumplings, 131
Cockie Leekie, **129**
Cocktails:
  bloody Maria, **145**
  bloody Mary, 51
  bullshot, **51**
  godfather, **153**
  Lolita, **145**
  Margarita, **145**
  tequila sunrise, **145**
  tequila sunset, **145**
Coconut, desiccated, 62, 128
Cod, 101:
  liver oil, 51
Coffee, 30, 43, 62, 99, 114, 122, 125,
  152, 154:

Blue Mountain, 150
instant, 152, 154
Coley, 6, 7
Confectionery:
  After Eight mints, 30
  caramel, 2
  Everton toffee, 2
  fudge, 2, 30
  Japanese, 140
  Jelly Babies, 30
  Liquorice Allsorts, 11, 128
  nut cracknel, 2
  Smarties, 30, 111
  toffee apples, 111
  Turkish delight, 2
Consommé, 42, 50
Cookery, writers on, 13, 24–5, 45–7:
  Beeton, Mrs, 24–6
  Boulestin, Marcel, 47–8, 125
  Brillat-Savarin, Antelme, 69, 82,
  112
  Carrier, Robert, 26
  Charles, Prince, 44
  Child, Julia, 46
  Costa, Margaret, 24
  David, Elizabeth, 24
  Harben, Philip, 47
  Heath, Ambrose, 125
  Larousse, 24, 84
  Leith, Prue, 24
Coq au vin, 4:
  House of Commons name for, 42
Courgettes, 11
Court bouillon, **101**
Crab, 161:
  dressed, 69, 166
Cranberries, 22:
  sauce, 165
Cream, 11, *37*, 44, 53, 13:
  clotted, 122–4
  curdled, *74*
  double, 25
  sour, 62, 132
  whipped, 101
Crème brûlée, 125
Crisps, 29, 36, 111, 152, 154
Croissants, *44*, 62, 114
Crumpets, 70, 73
Cuckoo, 57
Cucumber, 132:
  sandwiches, 25, 120

Curry, 38, 59, 140:
 tripe, 47
Custards, 1, 162

Dairy industry, 30
Darjeeling tea, 2
Devils on horseback, 166
Diets:
 fattening, 65–6
 slimming, 64–5
Dinner, 19, 120
Dips, 103
Doughnuts, 73, 160:
 for breakfast, 115
Dressing, 161
 see also Stuffing
Drinking hours, 112–4
Duck:
 Peking, 53, 135–6
 roast, 65
 Szechwan, **136**
Duckling, 112.
Dumplings, 28–9
 roast, 65
 Szechwan, *136*
Dumplings, 28–9

Eating places:
 in London:
 Anna's Place, 108
 Chicago Pizza Pie Factory, 101
 Claridges, 115
 Coconut Grove, 101
 Connaught Hotel, 115
 Davy's wine bars, 122
 Grunt's, 101
 House of Commons, 40–2
 Lone Star Cafe, 41, 101
 Lyons Tea Shops, 125
 Paper Tiger, 137
 Red Lion, Waverton Street, 95
 Savoy Hotel, 115
 elsewhere:
 Manchester: Midland Hotel, 115
 New York: Sherry Netherland
  Hotel, 115
 Scotland: Gleneagles Hotel, 115
 Whittlesey: Falcon, 108
 Windsor: Measures tea rooms, 122
 Wisbech: White Lion, 108
Eau de vie de Framboise, 49, 63

Eggs, 10, 70, 116; to peel, 5:
 and bacon, 114
 Benedictine **62**, 115
 and chips, 30
 fried, 146
 gulls', 152
 hard-boiled, 24, 111, 132
 poached, 15, 166
 quails', 11
 scotch. 36, 119
 scrambled, **126**
Elevenses, 62

Fish, 118; to marinade, 39:
baked, **133**
 boiled, 15
 brawn, 108
 cakes, bought, 98
 and chips, 107, 135, 138, 147
 fingers, 16
 Japanese, 138
 smoked, 132
 stale, 38
 see also under varieties of
Flour, 17, 26:
 millers, 30
Fondu, **49**:
 Bourguignon, **49**
Forcemeat, 28
Freezer, use of, 120
Frosties, 150
Fruit:
 crystallised, 44
 Marks and Spencer's, 36
 old, 39
 pie, *37*, 162
 salad, 10, **26**

Game pie, 132
Gammon, *93*
Garlic, 59:
 sausage, 116
Garnishes:
 definitions, 59–60
 not for cucumber sandwiches, 25
 objections to, 40–1
 radish and watercress for pâtés, 98,
  101
 sorrel for salmon trout, 112
 tomato and olives for sandwich
  loaf, 24

172

variety for Szechwan duck, 136
wild mushrooms for carbonnade, 56
Gateaux, 55
Gelatin, *39, 87*
Gherkins, 99, 103
Gin, 6, 7
Ginger, 80, *124*:
  ale, 151
  crystallised, 49, 64
Goose, 12, 163
Grape brandy, 6
Grapefruit, 62, 115, 161
Grape Nuts, 62, 115, *125*
Grouse, 130, 152:
  roast, 23, **62-3**
Guides:
  Michelin, 107-9
  Ronay, 109, 158
Guinness, 66

Haddock, 101, 130
Haggis, **129**
Ham, 24, 35, 72, 102, 158, 161, 162:
  Danish breakfast, 114
  English regional, 160
  and potato salad, **104**
Hamburgers 30, 56, 58, **140-3**
Herbs, 13, *37*, 62
Herring, 161:
  for breakfast, *130*
  salted, 132
Hock, 7
Hollandaise sauce, 4, **14**, 130:
  House of Commons name for, 40
Honey, 25, 150
Horlicks, 110
Hot dog, 140

Ice-box, to construct, 153
Ice-cream, 33, 98, 111, 140:
  blueberry, 41
  in Japan, 137
  lemon, **76**
  peach melba, 60
  sauces for, **98**
  vanilla, 60
Isinglass, 2

Jam, 22, 53, 130:
  Chivers, 22
  Co-op, 22

Elsenham, 23
English Provender, 23
Hartley's, 22
Mrs Bridge's, 23
Robertson's, 22
strawberry, 25, 125, **131**
Tiptree, 23, 124, 131
Jellies, 1

Kail, 130
Kangaroo tail soup, 140
Kedgeree, 94, 102, 126, **127**
Ketchup, 44, 141, 142,
Kidneys, 126:
  lamb's on toast, **149**
Kippers, **114**:
  fillets, 120
  mousse, 126
Kir, **63**
Kirsch, in jam, 23
Kiwi fruit, 26
Kulibiaki, **133**
Kumquats, 44

Lamb: to marinade, **38**:
  cutlets, 42, 53, 125
  kidneys on toast, **149**
  roast, 61, 108, 162
Laurent Perrier, 109-10
Leeks, 15, 129, 152
Lemon, 41, 74-6:
  cake, 2
  curd, 25
  ice-cream, **76**
  juice, 14, *37*, 65, 92
  peel, 7
  syrup, **26**
Limeade, 43
Limes, 143, 144
Liqueur: 23, *37*
Liquorice, 2, 128
Liver, 70
  chicken with bacon, 103
  goose, 92
  hotpot, **88**
Lobster, 161:
  mousse, 166,
  Newburg, *60*
  risotto, 102
  salad, 132
  Thermidor, 43

Loganberries, 130
Lunch (eon), 19, 47, 125:
  buffet, 36
  ploughman's, 117
  Victorian, for MP, 42–3

McDonald's, 53, 93, 137
Mace, 96, 103
Mackerel, **54**, 161
Mangoes, 161
Margarine, 6, 13, 22, 37
Marinades, **38**, **39**, 100, **156**
Marks and Spencer, 35–6, 66, 150, 165
Marmalade, 12, 62, 74, 114, 116, 130, **166**
Marmite, 73
Mayonnaise, 24, 45, **87**, 111, 130, 161
  fennel, 147
  for cold fish, **101**
Mazurka, 134
Meat loaf, **133**
Meat pies, 72
Melon, Ogen, 26, 154, 161
Milk, 62, 65, 115, 124, 125, 150
Milkshake, 33:
  banana, **68**
  grown-ups', **149**
Minestrone alla fiorentina, 53
Mint, 22
Moselle, 7
Mousse, savoury, **53–4**
Mousseline sauce, 4, 130
Muesli, 55
Muffins, 115
Mulligatawny soup, tinned, *44*
Mushrooms, 59, 132:
  for breakfast, *116*, 126
  grilled, 28
Mussels, 161
Mustard, *37*, 44, *76–8*, 103, 111, 119, 126, 143, 165

Noodles, for breakfast, 115
Nouvelle cuisine, 11, 41, 92, 93, 99, 100

Oatcakes, 131
Olives, 29, 116
Omelette Arnold Bennett, *60*
Onion, to peel, *5*
  fried, 56

Oranges:
  junket, 108
  Seville, 12, 152
Oxo, 72
Ox tongue, 71, 72
Oysters, *63*, 69, 152, 161
  stuffing, **162**

Paella, 140, 153, 154
Paines (brewers), 117
Pancakes, 135, **136**
Papaya, 161
Paprika, 2
Parsley, *37*, 129:
  as garnish, 41
Partridge, 6, 30, 158
Pasta, **98**, 140, 149
Pastry:
  English, 71–2
  flaky, 2
  puff, 49, 112
Pâtés, 95–6, 97, 126, 161
Peaches:
  in Melba, *60*
  liquidised, **62**
Peanut butter, 21
Peanuts, 29, 103, 111
Peas, 11, 59, 125
Petits fours, 30, 31
Pheasant, 152, 158, 159, 165:
  kedgeree, **94**, **127**
  pie, 159
Philadelphia Cream Cheese, 54
Pickles, 44, 72, 99
Picnics, 47, 152–4
Pimms No. 1, **151**
Pineapple candied, 100
Piroshki ('little pie'), **133**
Pizzas, 73, 161
Plover's eggs, 6
Plums, 23:
  brandied, 23
  in black chocolate, 44
  preserve, 2
Poire William, 64
Polish Pure Spirit, 110
Pommes soufflés, 63
Pork:
  belly of, 99
  cheese, 125, **126**
  and grouse pâté, 23

pies, 35, 36, 118
roast, 94, 123
salt, 112
sweet and sour, 135
Port, *4*, 64
Potatoes, 5:
  baked, 62, 119, **121–2**
  mashed, 133
  new, 15, *64*, 93, **101–2**, 125, **126**
  salad, 71, **104**
  soup, 112
  steamed, 10
  with dill, 132
  pot roast, **29**
Prawns, 161:
  cocktail, *40*
  Dublin Bay, 103
Preserving, various methods, 38, 166
Prunes, 129
Public houses, 34, 113, 116–9
Puddings, 69, 111, 123, 126, 162:
  bread and butter, 44, 69
  Christmas, 129
  Marks and Spencer's, 36
  roly poly, 22
  soggy bread in, 28
  summer, **148**
  tapioca, 31
  tinned, 55
Pumpkin pie, 101, 161

Quail's eggs, 11
Quiche, 103, 162

Radishes, 30, 132
Raspberries, 23, 30, 60, 130
Ratatouille, *64*, **70**
Redcurrant jelly, 165
Reindeer, 163
Restaurants and caterers, 28, 30, 31,
    40–1, 92, 105–7, 110
Rice, 50, 135, **157**
Rice Krispies, 48, 115
Risotto, 102

Sago, 6, 7
Salads:
  lettuce and walnut, **143**
Marks and Spencer's ready-prepared,
    36
  rice, **157**

watercress and corn, **63**
Salami, 114, 132
Salmon, 130, 161:
  Canadian frozen, **101**
  raw, 139
  smoked, 30, 65, 122, 154
  trout, **39**, 152
Sancerre, 63
Sandwiches, 21, 70, 72, 122
  bloater paste, 152, 154
  cucumber, 25
  egg and watercress, 159
  fish paste, 154
  ham, 35, 37
  loaf, **24**
  old cheese, 158
Sangria, **154**
Sardines, 21, 24
Sauces:
  barbeque, **157**
  bread, **164**
  chaufroid, *147*
  for prawn cocktail, **40**
  Hollandaise, 4, **14**, 40, 140
  mayonnaise, 24, 45, **87**, **101**, 111,
    130, 147, 161
  mousseline, 4, 130
  ravigotte, 3, 158
  Tapps, **167**
  white, 12
Sauces, proprietary:
  Brand's A1, 13, 85
  Daddy's, 13
  Escoffier Cumberland, 98
  Flag, 13
  Hellmann's mayonnaise, 86
  HP, 13
  Tabasco, 46
  Worcestershire, 84, 167
Sauerkraut, 140
Sausages, **103–4**, 111, **148**, 156, 161,
    164:
  for breakfast, *116*, 126
Scallops, 161
Scones, 25, **123–4**, **131**
Sea bass, 139
Seaweed, 139
Seltzer, 7
Semolina, 46, 117, 134
Sercial, 1
Seven-Up, 151

Sheep's head galantine, 125
Sherry, *4, 44*, 99:
  trifle, 56
Shortbread, Scots, 131
Shrimps, potted, 40
Slimming, 64
Smetana, 132
Smoking, 8, 39, 90–1:
  cigars, 70
Snoek, 30
Snuff, 144
Soda, 143
Sole, 161:
  Véronique, 59
Sorbets, 55
Soup, 50, 147, 159:
  chicken and vegetable, **12**
  hamburger (hefty), 141–2
  keeping, *39*
  Mulligatawny, *44*
  schi, 132
  tinned, *44, 67*, 97
  tomato, 46, **47**
  turtle, 125
  vichyssoise, *44*, **97, 147**
  with noodles, 48
Spam, 95
Spare ribs, 73
Spinach, 59
Steak:
  sukiyaki, 138
  tartare, 84–5, 132
  teriyaki, 138
Stew, 102, 103, 147
Stirrup cup, 1
Strawberries, 60, 152:
  jam, 25, 124, 131
  pulp, 22
  soufflé, 49
  wild, 63
Stuffing:
  chestnut, **165**
  for turkey, **82, 165**,
  oyster, **162**
Suckling pig, 63
Sugar, 7, *13*, 62, 99, 115, *124*, 125
Sultanas, 111, *124*
Summer pudding, **148**
Swedes, 130
Syrup of figs, 51

Tapioca, 32
Tarragon, 3:
  chicken, **80**
Tea (beverage), 2, 62, 70, 124, 125, 127:
  China, 120–1
  Japanese, 138
Tea (repast), 19, 25–6, 47, 120–2
  cream tea-rooms, 107
Tempura, 138
Tequila, 143–5
Timaale des oreilles de cochon, sauce ravigotte, 3
Toast, 21, 97, 114, 126: methods of
  making, 28:
  chanterelles on, **64**
  for Welsh rarebit, 27–8
  kidneys on, **149**
  Melba, **60**
Tomatoes, 59, 126:
  salad, 98
  soup, 46, **47**, 67
Tourin aux tomates, **47**
Treacle, 129
Trout, 161
Truffles:
  in forcemeat, 63, 92
  in puff pastry, 48, 112
  slivered, 44
  white, 6
Turbot, 161
Turkey, 22:
  boiled, **82**
  hanging, 82
  products, 81
  roast, 161–2, **163–4**
Turnips, 130:
  au gratin, 151

Ugly fruit, 161

Vanilla, essence of, 19
Veal and oyster 'dressing', 162
Venison, 130, 163
Vichyssoise soup, **147**
  tinned, *44*, **97**
Vitamin pills, 51, 53
Vodka, 144, 147

Waffles, 150–1:

for breakfast, 115
Watercress and corn salad, **63**
Welsh rarebit, **27**, 105
Whisky, 42–3, 53, 102, 129, 130,
  143, 144
Wine, 1, *4*, 65, 94:
  Chinese, 136
  for children, 110

mulled, **12**

Yams, 162
Yeast (*saccharomyces*), 16, 17
Yogurt, 55:
  for breakfast, 114

Zanuski, 132